Honest to God

Psalms for Scribblers, Scrawlers, and Sketchers

JAMES C. SCHAAP

FAITH ALIVE®
Christian Resources

Grand Rapids, Michigan

Printed in the United States of America.

We welcome your comments. Call us at 1-800-333-8300 or email us at editors@faithalive resources.org.

Library of Congress Cataloging-in-Publication Data
Schaap, James C., 1948-
    Honest to God : Psalms for scribblers, scrawlers, and sketchers / James C. Schaap.
        p. cm.
    ISBN 978-1-59255-526-0
    1. Bible. O.T. Psalms—Meditations. I. Title.
    BS1430.54.S32 2010
    242'.5—dc22

                                                            2010039749

10 9 8 7 6 5 4 3 2 1

Contents

Preface

'm no theologian—let's get that on the table right away. I don't know Greek or Hebrew. I never took a seminary class, and I don't know much at all about the conventions of Hebrew poetry. What's more, if I were to walk two blocks east to the college library, I could find a shelf full of books on the Psalms, more than you or I could ever read. I'm no expert, and this book of meditations is not the last word on the Bible's most celebrated poetry.

Hanging on the wall just above my computer, a framed diploma documents the fact that I have a graduate degree in the study of literature, but I'm not sure a degree helps all that much. I'm quite confident, in fact, that God, in his infinite wisdom, doesn't believe literary scholars are any better at reading his Word than the butcher, the baker, or the candlestick maker. After all, look what Jesus said about kids and their faith.

But I am a child of the Protestant Reformation, enough, at least, to believe that the Scriptures belong to all of us, and especially to those who have ears to hear and who love the Lord God Almighty, the Creator of heaven and earth—the God who has given us what Eugene Peterson calls "The Message." Once upon a time the open Bible was positioned in church sanctuaries in such a way that only priests had access to its contents. The Reformation—and Johannes Gutenberg—changed all that. Some congregations keep an open Bible at the front of the church, facing not the clergy but the people. The Reformation made life for believers decidedly more democratic. Power to the people.

Way back in grade school, Christian grade school, this Protestant kid was taught that reading the Word and studying it was both a joy and a way of life. That massive book, I came to believe, offers precious truths central to living a joyful, blessed life.

I'm older now, and not quite so sure that understanding God's Word is as easy as I was once told or thought. Oh, the truth is still there, the truth once summarized for me by an old friend who said that the whole story of the Bible is quite simple: we continually mess up, but God somehow loves us anyway. As a rule book for life, the Bible offers guidance all right, but not as propositionally—"Do this, don't do that"—as I once thought.

I've remained a kid who believes in the Word. I believe that reading it, studying it, thinking about it is not only eternally beneficial but very much a blessing here and now. That is to say, reading the Bible will not only help you and me gather some strong sense of our eternal destinies, it will also help us steer our way through the abundant and sometimes perplexing creation the Creator loves so much and gave us for our joy and his praise. This world is a vale of tears all right, but it's also a wonderland.

The Bible—and the Psalms—are instructive. No doubt. But it seems to me we're fooling ourselves if we believe we'll ever understand it or them fully (whatever *fully* means). When I was a kid—say, sixth grade or so—my favorite biblical passage was the one where Christ beckons us: "Come to me. . . . Take my yoke upon you and learn from me" (Matthew 11:28-29). Honestly I didn't have a clue what that meant when I was twelve. I think I know better today. The Bible hasn't changed but—trust me on this—from six to sixty, I have.

But then, understanding what the Bible says is not a one-time moment. Understanding both God's Word and our response to it is a pilgrimage that reaches its ordained destination at the Celestial City some day, and not here on *terra firma*. So let's be clear: nothing I say in these meditations is authoritative or scholarly, certainly not definitive. What I say is what these absolutely precious lines of holy poetry make me envision.

Throughout my life I've found that writing out what I think is a powerfully healthy exercise. A man named Abraham Kuyper taught me some things about writing devotions. I didn't know him, of course; he was dead long before I was born. He was once Prime Minister of the Netherlands, a prolific writer and journalist in addition to being a politician and a clergyman. Thousands of people of my tribe—the Dutch Calvinists—came to North America as immigrants in the last century toting books by Kuyper.

One of those books, *To Be Near Unto God*, was a much-beloved favorite among my ancestors. Years ago, I started reading that book and then decided to revise it to make it more "contemporary." When I did, I learned something about the way Abraham Kuyper operated as a devotional writer. To me Kuyper seemed to be something of a jazz musician when it came to meditation. Comparing nineteenth-century Dutch Calvinists to jazz musicians is a stretch, I know—worth a hearty giggle, in fact. But I swear it's true. When Kuyper took hold of a text, he took off on a riff the way a blues saxophonist might do. He let loose. He let himself go, let himself think, let himself dream. He ambled around the scriptural territory, finding his way eventually to real meaning.

That's what I'm doing in these meditations, and that's what I'm asking you to do—just riff.

One more thing. I've been teaching writing for my whole professional life, while doing a good bit of it myself—writing, that is. Southern writer Flannery O'Connor once claimed that she really didn't know what she thought about things until she put pen to paper. "I don't know so well what I think until I see what I say," she once wrote to a friend. "Then I have to say it over again." To most of the writers I know, that makes perfect sense. It's a kind of creed. In all truth, writing is—for me and for many others—a way of knowing.

Now listen to the teacher. Read the passage, read the meditation, and then scribble down whatever that prompts from your heart and head and soul. Doing that will help you make sense of things. Trust me. Better yet, trust Flannery O'Connor.

Have fun. Be real. This isn't Bible study, and you don't have to bounce things off someone else or wonder whether your thoughts pass muster. You don't have to listen to some other fool's prattle. Neither did David the king, David the poet. I believe that one of the reasons God Almighty claimed that David was a man close to his heart was because David was always in conversation with his Lord, no matter what his mood. Sometimes he raised his hands in praise; other times he raised his fists in anger. The psalms teach us that God Almighty has really thick skin. So trust God's largesse and love, and just write.

Let 'er riff!

Blessings,

James Calvin Schaap

Knowing Myself

All men should strive to learn before they die
what they are running from, and to, and why.

—*James Thurber*

‡

There is no one on earth who is righteous,
no one who does what is right and never sins.
—Ecclesiastes 7:20

‡

Stronghold

‡

The salvation of the righteous comes from the LORD;
he is their stronghold in time of trouble.

—Psalm 37:39

‡

I admit it. I've never taken much of a shine to the praise team phenomenon—four or five people from the congregation standing up and leading the singing. It's no burning issue with me, and I get along just fine every Sunday when a new praise team stands up and does its thing. I'm just saying I could easily do without.

Last night in a bigger auditorium the praise team was greatly enlarged, maybe twenty folks strong. I liked that, perhaps because with more of them singing they were a forest, not just trees—if that makes any sense.

Several of them were kids, two or three of them too young to know the words to most of the music. But they knew one song, an old children's song I hadn't heard for a bunch of decades. I don't know if the song has a title, but it's about the parable of the house built upon a rock: "The wise man built his house upon a rock (*repeat three times*) . . . and the house upon the rock stood firm." Boom. End of verse. That kind of firm.

In case you don't know it, the next verse compares the efforts of the foolish man who built his house upon the sand: once the rains fell, his sad shack went "splat." I didn't remember a "splat" when I was a kid—the song's been updated these days for more oomph. There are actions too—lots of pounding because there's lots of building.

The final chorus made *me* go "splat": "The blessings come down as the prayers go up (*repeat three times*) . . . so build your life upon the Lord."

It's so blasted easy, so childlike. It's like first-grade math, when everything still makes sense: the more we pray, the more we're blessed. Need more goodies, just bow your head. Prosperity is guaranteed for those who supplicate.

Honestly, the spiritual transaction the song offers as verifiable, biblical truth simply isn't as easy to buy as it is to sing. And it certainly wasn't yesterday.

Those of us who know depression know that blessings just don't descend or arise that simply. If I could tally the prayers we've given in the last several years—and I know others who have suffered far longer—my closet would overflow, I swear. But yesterday, while we were singing that little children's ditty, some people I know and love were off very much on their own, still looking frantically for themselves in what seems to be utter darkness, and I don't have the strength to build a house. What's more, I shouldn't, because sure as anything I'm standing on sand.

Years ago, in the Superstition Mountains of Arizona, I remember hiking to a place called "Cochise's Cave," a stronghold the old Apache chief used more than a century ago. Standing there, I had a very clear sense of what it meant to think of God Almighty as a fortress, a stronghold, even a rock—all of that real psalm language. From Cochise's Cave, you could see for miles, and nobody could sneak up. Trust me, any fugitive could get some great shut-eye in Cochise's Cave. So often in the psalms, that's where David says he is—at home in the rock that is the Lord.

I know a stronghold when I see it, when I'm in one.

But it's just not as easy as 1-2-3 or as fun as a praise team.

How does the line go? "I believe, Lord; help my unbelief."

Prayer

The truth is, Lord, there are times when the darkness simply doesn't admit much light, even though we beg and beg and beg. Don't hide from us. Please don't turn away. Be that brilliant porch light shining on our path. Keep us in your hand, your stronghold, especially when it seems as if we've been so terribly left behind. Amen.

Riff

Just exactly what don't you believe? Or when don't you believe?

Just a Few Smiles

‡

Make us glad for as many days as you have afflicted us,
for as many years as we have seen trouble.

—Psalm 90:15

‡

For three days, the child bled profusely from the nose. She was six years old, and doctors had no idea what was causing the bleeding. What's more, they understood that if the bleeding didn't stop, her life was in grave danger.

It was 1913. The doctors knew little about transfusion, but they did understand the importance of somehow getting good new blood back into the little girl's system, so they asked her father to give his daughter some of his blood. He did—it was one of the first transfusions in the state of Michigan. The yellowed newspaper story is titled, "Minister Saves the Life of Daughter by Giving Blood." It ends by explaining that the father "was considerably improved and was able to dress," adding, "The child was also considerably better and hopes are entertained for her recovery."

Two weeks later she was dead. Little Agnes Gertrude, my grandparents' oldest child, succumbed once the hemorrhaging returned. For a time her father's blood had brightened her face and her possibilities, but his gift—as unusual and strange to the newspaper readers as it must have been to him—wasn't sufficient to save her life.

Family lore says the doctors knew nothing about blood-typing at the time. Her father, my relatives speculate, was as good a choice as the doctors could have made, but he was not a match. Agnes Gertrude, my aunt, died two weeks after that strange new procedure the doctors called transfusion.

I have no newspaper accounts of my grandparents' grief, but I know some oral history. Agnes's little sister told me how her father lay face down on the rug of the living room for almost a week after Agnes's death, as if unable to move. She told me he was lethargic, depressed, his whole countenance darkened by the death of his child.

Nothing changed, she said, until he accepted a call to another congregation, a small country church up north. She told me how she remembered riding up to that country church on a wagon, the family's possessions packed up behind them, and being greeted by the entire church, waiting on the lawn for the new preacher and his family.

"That was it," she told me. The darkness ended.

I can't imagine it was completely over. If my grandparents were still alive, I'd like to be able to ask them about their loss, if they could talk about it. But in the eyes of their five-year-old daughter, the one who told me the story at least seventy-five years later, the darkness ended that summer day on the lawn of a country church full of welcoming people.

I wonder how someone like my grandfather, the preacher, read a verse like this one from Psalm 90. He must have read it a hundred times at a hundred funerals. I wonder what he thought of its modest petition: "Lord, give us as many days as you do nights, as much joy as sorrow, as many smiles as tears. That's all we're asking."

Spurgeon says the question is dear because it's childlike. Maybe he's right. I'm not sure. What it is—and thank God Almighty for it—is human. It's so understandable, so obviously wrenched from a mournful heart.

Once in a while, just let us laugh, Lord—we're not asking for much.

Is it any wonder why people love this psalm?

Prayer

Most of our lives have a whole lot more than we ever could have hoped for, and yet maybe a whole lot less too. In joy and in sorrow, keep us close to you, Lord. Help us not to rely on our own strength, but to put our trust in you. Amen.

Riff

It doesn't seem like much to ask, really—an equal number of good and bad days, of sorrows and joys, of grief and triumph. Think of three or four on either side of the ledger. Does it still seem like much to ask?

The Years of Long Ago

I thought about the former days, the years of long ago. . .

—Psalm 77:5

‡

O nce upon a time, a tenant farmer worked some land in an obscure county in an obscure state. Wasn't good land, at least not by his neighbor's reckoning. The soil was light and thin. Useless bluffs, lots of them, shouldered a river that all too often flooded the valley beneath. He rented that land from a man who had determined that most of what he'd made during his life would be given, upon his death, to a hospital not far away.

Along came the Depression, according to this yellow sheet of newsprint that tells the story. The landlord mortgaged his land to the hilt to keep from losing it, but when he died mid-Depression, that hospital became a landlord.

To say times were tough is understatement. In this corner of the world, it was smarter to shoot cattle than feed them, if you had any cattle at all.

When things grew desperate, the renter went to the hospital board and asked for grace—a thousand dollars' worth of rent simply couldn't be had and consequently couldn't be paid. The board graciously gave their consent.

Those hills nobody else wanted? They ended up being the heart of the family's survival. When drought meant no feed could be grown or purchased, the renter let his sheep graze the bluffs, where they ate the buck brush. When things got even bleaker, he shooed his hogs up there to munch acorns from the strips of burr oak that ran like an unruly mustache over the hills. While other farmers were dumping livestock, those unwanted bluffs saved the operation, and by the time the Second World War came around, the family farm got on its feet.

This old newspaper clipping is from 1976, some forty-four years after the hospital board nodded their collective heads and let that thousand-dollar rent payment ride. An old guy stands in the picture, his shirt buttoned up tight beneath his chin. To his left is his wife, wearing a hair net and a print jacket, a mother-of-pearl brooch perfectly centered on her chest. The man is handing a piece of paper to a big guy with an open collar. It's a thousand dollars. All three are smiling, forty-four years later.

Like I said, I have the yellowed scrap of newsprint to prove it. I'm saving it because this obscure story—otherwise long-forgotten—

21

needs to be remembered for our time and all time. It's a story about integrity.

I've always been a sucker for nostalgia, for the warm glow that remembrance of things past can sometimes offer us. I don't think I'm a fool. I'm not assuming that people paid back long-forgotten debts regularly back then. I have always had a Calvinist's sense of human nature.

But sometimes it's hard not be wistful, and good old stories, whether or not we were a part of them, can fortify us. I for one would argue that stories do more than laws to make us good. When the psalmist Asaph looks back, whatever it is he remembers argues for God's love, even in what seems to be his God's absence.

"Once upon a time . . ." he tells himself. He remembers, and he's strengthened. That's why I won't just toss this old news story, faded though it may be.

Prayer

There is no golden age, Lord—we know that. But some things—often some little things that happened long ago—are worth remembering, not just for who did them, but for why and how. We thank you for those who've done the right thing. May we not forget the good things, and may we pattern our lives by love. Give us the heart and soul to create good memories. Amen.

Riff

Sometimes it seems harder to do the right thing than not. Got any good stories?

Green Pastures

He makes me lie down in green pastures. . . .
—Psalm 23:2

‡

I only wish he'd do it more often.

Almost thirty years ago, when I took a teaching job at the school where I've been teaching ever since, a whole gang of my colleagues (including me) would walk over to the college coffee shop twice a day—that's right, twice a day—for a half-hour break. That was a quarter-century ago, about the time Edison first lit the incandescent bulb. No one in my department has daily coffee today.

Last Saturday our church held its annual fall cleanup. A whole bunch of us get together to wash windows, clean gutters, vacuum Sunday school rooms, do whatever, and "fellowship." I ripped up a moldy basement rug, and, for most of the day, ate the grainy black dust I scraped up from the floor beneath that shoddy carpet.

I didn't "fellowship" all that much, in part because I was ornery. I felt as if I *had* to go to cleanup day, and my time is precious. I'd much rather have paid somebody else to lift that carpet because, like most people I know, I have far more money than time.

I'm busy—who isn't? I still drink coffee, but my cup sits on a little electric hot pad beside my computer in the confines of my office. I haven't been to the coffee shop this year, not once, and the semester is drawing to a close.

I don't lie down in green pastures. Goodness knows I wouldn't have to look far; in fact, I know a couple of acreages that look downright inviting. But what I want to know is, who's got that kind of time?

I know this verse is metaphor. I know David the poet is just stretching the comparison into a conceit: because the Lord is my shepherd, he makes me (like a sheep) lie down on sweet green grass. I know he doesn't mean it literally, and, trust me, I'm not throwing a tent up next weekend. In Iowa it's almost winter.

I wonder whether anyone ever thought of the sheep here as a victim. After all, there's verifiable coercion in the verse. Psalm 23:2 does not say, "I lie down when I feel like it." Instead, David joyously claims, "he makes me lie down." That's why I say, I wish he'd do it more often. I wish the Lord would put me down on some sweet green grass—maybe even once a week. OK, once a month.

It sounds kind of dangerous. How many people don't I know who've said, after a hernia or a blown knee or even a bad head cold, that they would never have guessed they could exist for three days (or more!) in bed? Sometimes the Lord does, in fact, make us lie down.

But David's not simply remembering a vicious bout of the flu in Psalm 23. What he's saying is that the Lord Almighty takes care of him; he makes him lie down. He shows David some fine places and settles him in. He takes care of him.

Me too—a "Schaap" whose name actually means "sheep." He takes care of me. He makes me lie down in green pastures even when I don't think of it. He takes care of me even when I don't ask him. He shepherds me even when I don't shepherd myself.

I think I may have stumbled on to something. The Lord God Almighty cares for me. He loves me even when—my life seemingly out of control, far too busy—I don't care about myself enough to smell the roses or the fresh green grass.

Point me, Lord, toward the nearest pastures—winter or not. Make me lie down. Care for me in this spinning world of cares and pleasures. Love me as you promise.

Prayer

Sometimes we wish you would make us lie down, Lord. Sometimes we work far too hard, too many hours, putting far too much emotion into our jobs. Whenever that happens, Lord, put us down, make us sit for a while, show us your beauty, make us quit. Amen.

Riff

Years ago, schools switched from "physical education" to recrea-
tional sports because people believed that in the future we would
work less. Why do you think that never happened?

The Deeds of the Lord

Psalms for Scribblers, Scrawlers, and Sketchers Psalms for Scribs
Psalms for Scribblers, Scrawlers, and Sketchers Psalms for
Psalms for Scribblers, Scrawlers, and Sketchers Psalms for

‡

I will remember the deeds of the LORD;
yes, I will remember your miracles of long ago.
—Psalm 77:11

‡

Maybe a month ago I looked outside the rectangular window up at the ceiling (I'm in the basement) and saw the first robin I'd seen since last fall. It was perched precariously on a skeletal branch of the ornamental apple tree just off our deck.

A week later, no more, when I left the house in pitch darkness on my way to the gym, I heard the robin's song piping through the early morning.

A week ago, when I scratched away the detritus from the perennial bed, about a half-dozen green shoots, little triangular nubbins, were already steering their way up toward the light. Wherever I looked, there they were. I had to grub around a bit, but the mulch had done its job, creating a bed for infant buds slowly reaching toward the sun.

This morning there's no robin in the tree outside the window but the branches are festooned with hundreds of tiny purple explosions. The leaves are starting to bloom from those wiry, skeletal branches. My wife says that by the end of the week those scrawny branches will be full of life.

It's Easter, it's spring solstice, it's spring. The rivers are up, and the whole earthy world out here on the plains is mud-luscious. Yesterday it was eighty degrees, and the miracle of life is running in the sap that goes wild in trees and in young men and women (I live in a college town). The long, dark night of cold is history once again.

Amid the darkness he's documented in the early verses of Psalm 77, Asaph reminds himself to rehearse the miracles of his own people's grand narrative—Moses parting the waters of the Red Sea; life-bringing water from rocks; snakes raised up high in the wilderness. He wants to urge his doldrums away by putting some stock in the way the Egyptians wilted under the barrage of calamities—boils and bloody water, flies and pestilence and other assorted God-directed horrors. He tells himself to remember the immensely memorable stories of God's faithfulness, the miracles.

Each of us, it seems, can orchestrate our own repertoire of miracles: my mother's emotional incandescence after the death of my father, for instance. None of her children guessed that she would acclimate herself to life alone as grandly as she has. Her happiness and joy is a miracle, in a way—against and beyond all of our expectations.

It's not as showy, maybe, as an epidemic of frogs, as glorious as a release from generations of slavery, but for me it'll do for now. I can't remember, right off hand, any single event in my recent life that demonstrates supernatural interference in the normality of daily existence—I don't know anyone who didn't get on a plane that crashed or lived in a house that was miraculously saved in the path of some killer twister. But right now, with life itself arising from every square inch of ground outside, the budding trees full of birds, the air redolent with song—right now, spring itself is enough of a miracle to make me join the chorus.

"The miracles of long ago" are nothing to shake a stick at, but the ones happening in April's loving hands outside right now raise my own wilted spirits. It's spring, a taste of eternity. A miracle to witness.

Prayer

Give us grace to see the dawn, Lord, to see your divine nature in a crocus or a tulip, an ash or a willow. Give us vision to notice your miracles all around us, even in our own breath, since it's by your very Spirit that we live and have our being. Give us hearts big enough to let you in. Amen.

Riff

Spring is here. The miracle of life is returning. What other miracles might you be missing?

The Voice of the Lord

The voice of the LORD is powerful;
the voice of the LORD is majestic.
—Psalm 29:4

‡

I know wonderfully sincere Christians who describe conversations with God with language like this: "I wanted to write a book about dependency, but God told me he wanted me to write something else—something about relationships—and when I told him I didn't know much about relationships, he told me, 'I'll help you. Don't worry.'"

I have two reactions to such language—no three. First, why doesn't God speak to me that way? Am I a cracked vessel, or doesn't God really care what I'm up to? Maybe I need to listen in a wholly different way.

Second, what does the voice of the Lord sound like? I think of George Burns in *Oh, God*, the 1977 comedy in which George Burns as

God comes to a supermarket manager named Jerry Landers, played by John Denver. I liked the film, in part because Burns's character had a great sense of ironic humor. But God never seems to pull my friends' legs.

Third, isn't it a little arrogant to make such a claim, as if God Almighty sits aboard your shoulder like a macaw? Is that what God does?

Ralph Waldo Emerson resigned his pastorate when he decided that the Lord's Supper was a kind of idolatry. That one human being—a Jewish ascetic named Jesus—had given it eternal significance meant little or nothing at all to a nineteenth-century transcendentalist like himself. If Emerson were to hear God's voice, he'd hear it for himself, thank you. Revelation from the divine Oneness, he said, is an intuition. It cannot be received secondhand. What a sweet dreamer Waldo was!

How does God speak to us? There's another question for the ages. Old Testament Jewish life was littered with prophets who were cocksure they were getting their proclamations straight from the Source. Some were right; the vast majority were dead wrong. Jim Jones, a self-proclaimed spiritual conduit and founder of the People's Temple, created mass suicide in 1978 by ascribing his visions to the divine truth.

In Psalm 29, David creates a litany using the phrase "the voice of the Lord." He uses it six times in a row, each time with specific reference to a natural phenomenon any science teacher could explain away. Did you know that all around the world lightning strikes the earth about a hundred times per second? I didn't.

Is lightning really the voice of God? No more than a tornado, a tsunami, a volcano, or an earthquake. Many native people once worshiped the sun, in part because, without electricity, the darkness of night was downright scary.

So is David wrong? Is this just the rambling of a primitive, someone who made spiritual claims for perfectly explainable natural phenomena?

Here's my theory. One of the reasons God Almighty named David as someone close to his own heart was that the poet king never stopped communicating, never stopped listening to the still and solemn whispers within him, or the booming thunder on sleepless, stormy nights. King David saw God and heard him. What's more, he spoke intimately to the eternal eminence he couldn't fail to recognize every hour of his life.

I should be so good a listener, so reverent a communicator.

Prayer

Thank you for King David, Lord, and not just his poetry either. Thank you for giving him a voice to speak to you—to be angry, to be loving, to be penitent, to be everything any human can be. Thank you for his example of never letting you get far away. Keep us close too. Keep us talking. Amen.

Riff

David was constantly talking to God, constantly praying and praising. What might sometimes keep you from making that a practice too?

Day and Night

Psalms for Scribblers, Scrawlers, and Sketchers Psalms for Scrib
Psalms for Scribblers, Scrawlers, and Sketchers Psalms for
Psalms for Scribblers, Scrawlers, and Sketchers Psalms for

‡

Blessed are those who . . . meditate
on [God's] law day and night.
—Psalm 1:1-2

‡

I spend my day writing or teaching, mostly. Normally I watch about two hours of television, one hour of which is news. About an hour from now, I'll put in about thirty minutes at the gym and probably another thirty recovering. I'd rather not tally the time I spend piddling around, thereby avoiding the horrors of an empty computer screen. Honestly, it isn't all that much. I'm a Calvinist; we're the folks that gave the world capitalism, for heaven's sake. We make much of time.

What I don't do is meditate day and night on God's law. Not really.

Not long ago in an airport, I watched a man in a hat locate a private spot behind the ticket podium, take out some kind of cloth, unfold it carefully, and spread it out with remarkable precision. Then

36

he rolled up his sleeve and wound something that resembled black surgical tubing around his upper arm. He assumed some kind of position and started praying.

He was Jewish, strictly so, and he was meditating. Although he was discreet, his meditation was more public than, well, my meditation that evening. It was a prescribed ritual he felt was important to accomplish even though he wasn't at home. The ritual began and it ended; once we lined up to get on the plane the surgical tubing came off.

Because the psalms are poetry, we need to cut them a little slack when it comes to occasional bold assertions. I don't think anyone can take this statement—that the only way we can be blessed is if we meditate day and night—literally. In this case, my sense is that we need to respect the spirit of the law, not the letter of the law.

My great-grandfather, an eminent professor of theology, was notoriously absent-minded. One winter's day, as he was ruminating on some Bible text while skating down a Dutch canal on his way to preach at a church, someone grabbed him by the lapels in order to stop him from simply skating his way right into the open terror of the North Sea. Deep meditation, all right—it's fortunate he wasn't driving an SUV.

The strength of the English language is in strong verbs and concrete nouns—at least that's the rule. In this verse, however, I believe the finest truth is in a simple preposition—*in*. The King James Version has it, but Today's New International Version uses *on*, and while it may be more grammatically accurate, *on* seems to me to be North Sea dangerous.

Meditating *in* the law, day and night, leaves a lot of open space. Living *in* the law, living in God's covenant promises, suggests being in a world that allows space for writing and teaching as well as milking cows, selling cars, and holding apple-cheeked kids with too-high fevers, like I did just yesterday. Holding my sick grandson was a kind of meditation, just as writing this is.

I'd say it would be more accurate to say of Grandpa that he was meditating *on* the sermon than *in* it.

We all need spiritual discipline; we all need to talk with God. Failure to do so is to lose touch. But maybe, just maybe, we need to learn a little from our Islamic friends or our Lakota brothers and sisters. In a world where separation of church and state is a pillar of our national faith, we need to remember that all of life is spiritual, and that even our work is a meditation in God's law.

Prayer

In every moment of our lives, help us live in you, Lord. Help us live in meditation, live in your strength, your power, your love. Keep us near unto you. Amen.

Riff

Some of us know more chaos than discipline when it comes to staying in touch with the Lord. How can we do it better?

Righteous

Psalms for Scribblers, Scrawlers and Sketchers Psalms for Scrib
Psalms for Scribblers, Scrawlers and Sketchers Psalms for

✢

The ordinances of the LORD are sure,
and all of them are righteous.
—Psalm 19:9

✢

I remember reading somewhere that the word *righteous* has just about fallen out of standard usage. I'm sure you can hear the word in churches around the country, in meditations like this and other things "Christian," but on the street and in the workplace, the word is just about gone.

Not so *self-righteous*. That word has tons of currency and still sprinkles conversations hither and yon. But the virtual disappearance of the word *righteous* begs some interesting questions. Strange, isn't it? The word exists healthily in its contrary, but is almost extinct in its positive form.

I'm no etymologist, but I'm thinking that it doesn't take a scholar of the language to figure out why that's happened. Judging righteousness, after all, is a much tougher job than judging self-righteousness; in part, perhaps, because it's far easier to be self-righteous than it is to be truly righteous. I don't necessarily think there are more phonies around than there are good, good people. But I do know this: the people I might consider worthy to be described as righteous would likely be the first to tell you exactly the opposite.

In fact, one mark of the truly righteous is that they know deep within the sinews of their hearts that they are sinners. Which leads us back to the original claim—the truly righteous are the last to make any claim for righteousness.

It's probably fair to say to say that the word *righteous* works only when it's applied to someone else. "My Uncle George is a righteous man" is an assertion that feels acceptable to me. On the other hand, "I'm a righteous man" makes me raise an eyebrow.

Here, at the heart of David's final assertion about the Torah, or the way of the godly, or, as most commentators would say, the Word of God, the word *righteous* is used in a fashion that is perfectly correct. Here the word has nothing to do with humanity and everything to do with God's commands, his judgments throughout history, his Word.

If it appears that all around you there simply are no righteous to be found, to repeat the woeful claims of other psalmists; if it appears that those who consider themselves godly are really smarmy, fork-tongued loudmouths; if it seems sometimes that there is no justice in the world, that no one cares, that only the rich prosper, then,

David says, note this eternal truth: God's ways are sure, and all of them are righteous.

A week ago a bunch of college guys came over and roofed our house. The shingles were a mess, bent and torn, enfeebled by too many Iowa hailstorms. Before cutting some plywood, one of them pulled out a chalk line, marked out two spots on two edges of the sheet, then pulled that turquoise chalk line back like the string of a bow and snapped it down on the plywood, creating a perfectly straight line. He pulled out the circle saw and let fly, never doubting.

There was nothing crooked about it. The way of the Lord, David says, is something like that straight blue line.

Prayer

No one is truly righteous, Lord, no matter what anyone says. We all have sinned. We all have turned away. Thank you for coming for us when we're on our knees, Lord—thank you for loving us despite our unrighteousness. Only you are holy. Amen.

Riff

Write down the name of someone you think of as righteous. Why do you believe that about him or her?

Still Waters

‡

He leads me beside quiet waters.
—Psalm 23:2

‡

was thirty-two years old when someone at the Bread Loaf Writers Conference called to tell me that my application for a scholarship had been accepted, and they were offering me a position as a waiter. I had no idea what being a waiter meant, but I understood clearly from the conversation that the offer was a good, good thing.

The house where we lived at that time is long gone, as is the tiny kitchen where I stood, phone in hand, listening. The call had come in the middle of the day, in the middle of a meal. Our two little kids were sitting beside us.

It's now more than a quarter-century later, but I will never forget receiving that call because I had the distinct feeling that my being chosen for a waiter's scholarship to the granddaddy of all writers conferences, Bread Loaf, was a signal that fame and fortune lay just down the road. I had just published a book, my first, with a tiny local press, and now Bread Loaf beckoned. The *New York Times Book Review* was a year away.

When I flew into Burlington, Vermont, for the conference—early, because I was a waiter—I met a beautiful woman my age who said she was an aspiring poet. She was married, with two children. She'd also be a waiter. Someone from Bread Loaf picked us up, and we took the hour-long drive together into Vermont's Green Mountains. We made friends instantly.

Ten days later, when we boarded a plane to leave, she and I stood on the stairway to a small jet, waiting to enter the cabin. She looked at me and shook her head. "I hope this plane crashes," she said, and she meant it.

She'd been wooed by a celebrity poet, and she'd fallen. On the dance floor at night, the two of them looked like smarmy high school lovers, which might have seemed embarrassing if it hadn't happened to so many others. Another waiter—also married with kids, two of them—told me it was important for him to have an affair because, after all, as an artist he needed to experience everything in order to write with authority.

I am thankful to God for sending me to Bread Loaf, but it wasn't an easy place to be, for a waiter or anyone else, I'd guess. I'd lived most of my life in small, conservative communities that prided themselves on their churchgoing ways. Adultery was real, but a sad scandal; it wasn't commonplace.

The atmosphere in that mountaintop retreat was electric. Aspiring writers like me flirted daily with National Book Award winners, editors, agents, and publishers. From dawn until dawn we were always onstage.

I learned a great deal about writing at Bread Loaf, but much more about life itself and my place in it. In the middle of that frenetic atmosphere, on a Sunday morning, I walked alone out into a meadow, away from people, where I found a green Adirondack chair and sat for an hour, meditating. I tried to imagine what the soft arm of my little boy would feel like in my fingers; at the same time I recited over and over again the words of the 23rd psalm.

I remember a beautiful mountain stream, but no still waters at Bread Loaf Writers Conference in the summer of 1980. If there were any, I didn't see them. Even so, that Sabbath's very personal worship, right there in the middle of the madness, brought me—body and soul—to the very place David has in mind in verse 2.

I know still waters. God led me there.

Prayer

In the middle of all our tribulations, when almost everything around us seems at war with our spirit, when pain comes, or sadness—when tears fill our vision, lead us beside still waters, Lord. Take our hands and lead us on. Amen.

Riff

Can you think of a moment when it seemed as if God Almighty had sallied up and sat down right beside you?

.

Knowing God

There is a God-shaped vacuum in the heart of every man
which cannot be filled by any created thing, but only
by God, the Creator, made known through Jesus.

—Blaise Pascal

‡

This is what the Lord says—
Israel's King and Redeemer, the LORD Almighty:
I am the first and I am the last;
apart from me there is no God.
Who then is like me? Let them proclaim it.
Let them declare and lay out before me
what has happened since I established my ancient people,
and what is yet to come—
yes, let them foretell what will come.
Do not tremble, do not be afraid.
Did I not proclaim this and foretell it long ago?
You are my witnesses. Is there any God besides me?
No, there is no other Rock; I know not one.

—Isaiah 44: 6-8

‡

God's Laughter

‡

The wicked plot against the righteous and
gnash their teeth at them; but the Lord laughs at the wicked,
for he knows their day is coming.
—Psalm 37:12-13

‡

These days it seems that the victims of violent crime are given an opportunity in court, once the verdict is set, to speak to the guilty. It's not an exercise I enjoy watching. No matter how despicable and evil the crimes, those frequently emotional diatribes don't offer much joy. Venting may feel good but it's not pretty—vengeance in the human spirit, no matter how understandable, is almost always unbecoming.

Maybe if it was my daughter or grandson who was murdered, I would see it differently. Maybe if I'd suffered as some have, I'd want to take a few shots myself.

I hope and pray I never find myself in that position.

It's anthropomorphic, of course—this line in David's psalm. One can't help but get the impression that a smirking God is exactly the kind of deity David would like to believe in—after all, King David himself is getting his kicks at the inevitable plight of the wicked. The whole movement of this part of this psalm is to assert dramatically and unforgettably exactly how far the righteous stand apart from the wicked: the meek get joy and bounty; the wicked, gnashing their teeth, get hell. That's why God laughs. God knows what it's going to be like when he turns up the heat. It'll be a riot.

I love the image of God laughing, but David's description makes me uneasy, in part because God seems, well, almost disinterested—as if the drama unfolding in front of him is theater, as if he's actually entertained by what goes on in his creation. As if God's a season-ticketholder at the pageant of this world's foibles.

It's impossible to say that God doesn't do what David says he does in this verse, and therefore wrong to assume that this is simply poetic license. I know enough of God to know that I don't know it all. The Lakota idea of Wakan Tanka as "the Great Mystery" makes sense to me.

And because I'm human, I'm quite sure I could feel just like those murder victims' mothers and fathers and husbands and wives when they stand up to the victim's killer and let him (or her) have it. I know I could feel exactly what David does.

When the Allied liberators stumbled on the concentration camp at Dachau, the evidence of what had happened wasn't pretty. The skeletal prisoners—both the living and the dead—were such a horrifying shock to the liberators that ordinary soldiers became cold-blooded killers. There are reports of GIs giving prisoners their machine guns and simply allowing them to kill the hated Nazi guards. All of that—especially if you've seen boxcars loaded with corpses—is perfectly understandable. But was it right?

David's ascribing that human characteristic to God offers us—me included—some human joy. When I conceive of the Lord God Almighty acting just like me, it may well make it easier to like him. But it also makes is more difficult, I believe, to worship him.

I wonder if, in David's anthropological characterization of God, we're finding out more about King David, God's beloved, than we are God Almighty. I hope so. Because I really do hope that my God doesn't snicker at sinners.

Prayer

Dear Lord, what we know about you and what we don't know not only could but does fill whole bookshelves. We know your love because you've given us the Word made flesh, and we know, from the inside, Christ's great love for us. For that gift, our great thanks. Help us to love—even as your Son said—our enemies. Make us daily more like you. Amen.

Riff

Does God ever allow us our own measure of vengeance—or is vengeance always God's job, not ours?

Ordination

‡

The LORD makes firm the steps of those who delight in him;
though they stumble, they will not fall,
for the LORD upholds them with his hand.
—Psalm 37:23-24

‡

The rough logic of verse 23 of Psalm 37 is not difficult to understand: When—if ever—the Lord likes what he sees in a person, he gives that guy or gal a break. Sounds fair. That's the kind of God I can deal with. Like Wall Street, the Lord will love us if he determines we're worth the investment. I can deal with that.

But listen to this translation: "The steps of a man are established by the LORD," says the New American Standard; "and he delights in his way." Or the King James: "The steps of a good man are ordered by the LORD: and he delighteth in his way."

Correct me if I'm wrong, but in the gap that separates the translations, you could float a whale of a difference. In the TNIV above, something reciprocal is occurring—"You scratch my back, I'll scratch yours." As if God Almighty is shopping for a used car— kicking tires, checking mileage, looking for dings. If he likes what he sees, he buys. It's that simple.

In the King James, God isn't shopping. He's turning out human beings, setting them on a charted course and watching them go exactly where he's determined they would, as if, in a way, he were spinning tops. But even that's a lousy analogy, because, once the top is spun, the spinner has no idea of direction. Maybe he's like one of those folks who love model trains. Get the cars out of the box, assemble the tracks, and let 'em go.

What seems unmistakable in the King James and New American Standard is that God knows where we go, when we stand, and when we stoop, our ups, downs, and all arounds. What's more, God delights in watching it happen, in seeing what he, in fact, determined. He loves to watch us circle around the tracks he's laid.

That's a whole different God from the one looking for used cars—or so it seems.

At the base of the difference is a pair of contrary ideas that are not arcane, ideas that have puzzled human beings for centuries. Are we free agents, or is everything about us preconceived, foreordained, predestined? Good folks—brilliant theologians and learned scholars—have and will continue to disagree, I'm sure, as do, obviously, the linguists who work as Bible translators.

Who's right? Good question, and worth considering.

But what did the poet king say? Where would he come down? What did he intend? Whose translation is accurate?

Those questions don't bother me all that much because this is, first of all, a song and not an academic paper. Psalm 37 is all about security, about comfort, about feeling rest and peace in the Popeye arms of the One who made us and who never leaves.

In the very next verse David admits that he's an old man, a fact that may well be key to accepting the sheer joy of this line's thickly upholstered comfort. I'm probably about as old as he was when he wrote the song or offered the meditation. And I think I know why he wouldn't care for the debate. Really, there's just one thing David wants us to understand. When he looks back on his life—all of it—he knows deep down that the God who breathed his own breath into a child who would, surprisingly, become king, that God would never leave him alone. That God was there always and will be forever.

No matter how you read it, verse 23 is far less a proposition than it is a promise.

Prayer

Whether you are sovereign, Lord, whether you actually rule our lives and this whole wide world isn't a silly question because it helps us know better just who you are. But what we already know for sure about who you are is that you love, big-time, and you love us. Thank you for the comfort of your Word. Amen.

Riff

What good reasons do you give God to love you? Even if you can't think of any, does he love you anyway, all the time?

The Valley of the Shadow

‡

Even though I walk through the darkest valley,
I will fear no evil, for you are with me.
—Psalm 23:4

‡

Only once in my life have I walked through the darkest valley—the valley of the shadow of death—and that was just a few years ago when I sat for several days at the bedside of my father, who was dying. I knew it even though the doctors and nurses wouldn't say it and my family couldn't believe it—after all, what had brought him to the hospital was only searing back pain.

But I knew he wasn't going to get out of that bed on his own again because in the time I spent with him, he became less and less communicative. We never had a final talk, in fact. We never spoke in that blissful way most of us fantasize might occur in the final moments we share with those we love.

I helped him when he needed to drink, when he needed to urinate, when he felt deep pain; but honestly I don't think he knew I was there—or rather, who was there. The intensity of the pain and the effort his body was mounting simply to stay alive drew all of his strength and will and consciousness.

Only those who've been there will understand what I mean when I say that those days were among the best days of my life. Maybe things weren't said that could or should have been, and, sure, if I could rewrite the scene, I would. But I don't remember another time in our lives when I simply sat beside him, this man who gave me life itself and always loved me, even when I didn't deserve it.

A man came in one afternoon, a man from my father's church. I knew him from my childhood, but he wouldn't have been the man I thought the church might send. He was my father's district elder. It was his job, I know, to visit, and he did. When he came in, I told him my father likely wouldn't know he was there.

But my father's deliriousness didn't stop this visitor. This burly guy I remember as a truck driver walked up to the bedside, took my father's hand, and spoke to him as if my father understood every last word, tried to engage him in a conversation that didn't have a chance of starting. Once he realized that, this unlikely angel of mercy simply talked. He told my father that throughout his own life he'd always looked up to Dad. He told him how, as far as he was concerned, my father was one of those men he'd call truly godly. He told him how much he'd meant to him as a model of a Christian.

A big man with hair square as a GI, a guy I had trouble thinking of as an elder, a man I don't know I'd ever spoken to before—that man looked into my father's agonized face, held his hand, and told him in no uncertain terms that, as far as he was concerned, my father had modeled Jesus Christ in Oostburg, Wisconsin.

Then he backed away from my father's bed, looked at me, shook my hand, and left, wiping tears from his eyes.

I honestly don't know whether any of that got into my father's mind. I don't know whether he heard those words or picked up a hint of the warmth of the hand that held his. My guess is that he didn't, but I don't know. The nurses told me they'd often been surprised by what people in my father's condition did hear.

But I know I heard it—every single word of that truck driver's testimony—and I'm reminded of it now when I read this verse of this beloved psalm: "Even though I walk through the darkest valley, I will fear no evil, for you are with me."

That day, he sent a truck driver.

Prayer

Thank you, Lord, for blessings we don't see coming nor deserve. Thank you for sending a truck driver. Thank you sending a chocolate cake, a dozen daisies, a kiss on the cheek, a sweet letter from a former student. Thank you for immense blessings in ordinary packaging, gifts only you could send. Amen.

Riff

Sometimes God Almighty pulls off the most unexpected things. Think of one.

Stumbling

... though they stumble, they will not fall,
for the LORD upholds them with his hand.

—Psalm 37:24

‡

What Willa Cather experienced as a child on the Great Plains at the turn of the twentieth century, surrounded by a wave of recent immigrants, was something she never forgot and always celebrated. Her great pioneer novel, *My Antonia*, has given us one of the most powerful characters in American literature: Antonia Shimerda, a woman whose strength of character and purpose simply would not be defeated.

Antonia's was no easy life. During her first winter in America, when Antonia was still a girl, her father—an educated musician in his native Bohemia, a man clearly not fashioned for the hard work of opening the rugged prairie—took his own life one cold night.

Because he was a suicide, the local cemeteries wouldn't take his remains. The unpardonable sin at the time, it seems, was the despair Antonia's father suffered, the abandonment of hope itself, which is to say, the abandonment of faith. Mr. Shimerda, who shot himself in the barn, was buried in the road.

Willa Cather frequently drew her stories from her own experiences, and if you ever visit Red Cloud, Nebraska, the place where she grew up, you can follow dusty roads through the bleak and unforgiving landscape she loved, roads that go through places where she dug out the roots for some of her stories. Mr. Shimerda had a prototype on the land west of Red Cloud, and on one of those roads you can actually drive over the intersection where he was once buried, very much alone. It's an eerie feeling, even though the man's remains have long since been moved.

Today those who commit suicide are not refused burial in any cemeteries that I know of, and for that all of us can be thankful. I cannot sympathize a whit with those who kept Mr. Shimerda's body from a proper burial, but when I read a verse like this—from David—I can at least understand something of their fear, for fear is what it was. To take one's own life is to reject the eternal truth of what David says: "though they stumble, they will not fall, for the LORD upholds them with his hand."

Even though out here on the Plains we have come a long way from the horrible rejection of Mr. Shimerda and others like him, we still don't know quite what to do with those among us who take their own lives. We don't know what to do with them, in part, because those of us who are believers do know that the act of suicide defies the eternal hope of this verse and so many others from the Word of God.

Last week, in a community not far away, a man committed suicide. I didn't know him, never met him. But I know several members of his family, and I know of their profound grief. Since it happened, no one has said much about it because, well, there's not much to be said. By all accounts, the man was a believer. And he suffered badly for the past several years. I know very little else.

What I do know—what I believe, because I know this much of the Almighty—is that God alone will judge the living and the dead.

And I trust him. I trust God and his promises. I trust that God will do what he has always done and promises he will do forever—to love.

Prayer

Lord, sometimes we give up on those who give up. We've given up far too many times, in far too many stories. Help us to know how to love those who forget what it is to be loved. Help us to persevere as you do, to love without limit. Amen.

Riff

One of the characteristics of God—and not us—is that God continues love us, even when we're unlovable. Do you think that's overstatement?

All Mine

‡

I bring no charges against you concerning your sacrifices or
concerning your burnt offerings, which are ever before me.
I have no need of a bull from your stall or of goats from
your pens, for every animal of the forest is mine. . . .
—Psalm 50:8-10

‡

My wife just now called me upstairs because a cardinal, a bright red smudge against the snow on the branches of the evergreen, appeared as if out of nowhere.

I don't know if it should have been there. I don't really know a cardinal's seasonal flight plans, but all that crimson seems oddly out of place in the steely-cold dead of winter, just a few days from the solstice.

But what do I know?

Just now I read a loving little essay about the opossum, a marsupial I always assumed should be listed under "God's zaniest jokes." I don't know what the opossum contributes to the ecology of the neighborhood, but, unlike the cardinal, it sure isn't beauty. The writer, a fellow lover of the tall-grass prairie region where we live, tries to convince his readers that the opossum isn't as unsightly as people say. But who on earth would care to cozy up to something adorned with that absurdly pink nose or those strange eyes—not to mention that rat-like tail? Raccoons are cagey, minks are brilliant, but opossums are, well, mulish and half-dressed. They're as dumb as they look. And those fleshy toes are repulsive. That no one's ever made a horror movie out of a mutant opossum is surprising.

OK, OK—so they pouch their young. That's touching, I'll grant you that. And if you've got to meet any of God's furry nocturnals late some night, you could stumble on an opossum without suffering much damage. Unless cornered, they're as mild-mannered as Clark Kent, and they've been around forever, one of our oldest living mammals.

"We have many possums visit the ground beneath our bird feeders at night; sometimes as many as four," this friend of mine wrote in his online magazine. "Yet opossums are basically solitary animals and have separate territories, although they do not seem to squabble over the fact when their paths cross. An amiable trait if I do say so. They can hang around here all they want as far as I'm concerned."

I sent the writer a note telling him I wasn't persuaded, but maybe was a bit less critical. He told me he figured that was about as well as he could do. He's right.

Opossums are, of course, among God's wondrous creatures, among the company God himself brings up in this verse of Psalm 50. It's the opening volley of an argument that goes on for most of the rest of the psalm.

I've said it before—I live in one of the most prosperous cattle-feeding areas of this country, and hogs we've got by the hundreds of thousands.

Big deal, God says in this verse. I don't need your stock pens, your hog lots, your million-dollar confinements. I don't need your blessed sacrifice—I don't even need you. I've got opossums by the score, and it's all mine anyway, he says, all of these woods and this creation.

Out here, where a minute-and-a-half in any direction will set your feet in a cattle yard, believers like me may find it hard to remember the sacred character of the lowly opossum or a single pig.

But they all belong to God, who's the real landowner in these parts. No absentee either; God is very much here. Witness the glorious cardinal—and that lumbering bag of gray fur, the opossum.

All mine, God says.

Prayer

That you care for the opossums, that you watch over their world, that you have your eyes on the skunks, the weasels, and the lowly sparrows—all of that argues for your love, not only for us, but for your world. We sing, "This is my Father's world." Help us celebrate that very fact with our honor and praise. Amen.

Riff

From the time you were a child, has your attitude toward the environment changed? Why?

The Perfect Storm

The waters saw you, God, the waters saw you and writhed; the
very depths were convulsed. The clouds poured down water,
the skies resounded with thunder; your arrows flashed back
and forth. Your thunder was heard in the whirlwind, your
lightning lit up the world; the earth trembled and quaked.

—Psalm 77:16-18

✝

The days are thick and windless and unusually warm in
the morning. Humidity veils the sun's sparkle and casts
the whole world in a haze that glows, as if somewhere
down the road one could find a lake steaming in a section
of farmland. Some early summer days, every single afternoon sky
telegraphs an evening storm; each morning's stillness threatens, as
if dawn were only a ceasefire.

Out there in the atmosphere, pressure builds all day long until
gray-green thunderheads mass like a mountain range mirage and

rise slowly in the west, rolling upward into huge raised fists. Then it's just a matter of when and where and how violent.

The only way to live with tornadoes is to respect them from the moment they hint they could be brewing somewhere far away in a swirl of angry clouds.

One night, years ago, we rode out a storm in the cellar of our old house, a storm cellar built years ago—six inches of cement for a ceiling. Plenty of rain had fallen that spring, and the water table inched up so high that the hardware man joked there were only two kinds of people in town: the ones with water in their basements and liars. In our storm cellar water stood a couple of inches deep and there we sat—my wife with her robe hiked up above her knees, holding our daughter, her eyes like pocket watches in the dim glare of a naked forty-watt bulb set in the concrete wall. My pants legs were rolled up above my calves like pedal pushers, and we sat barefooted, ankle deep in rain water while outside the wind swept over like a Passover plague.

There was no tornado that night; we heard later that somewhere out on a farm a grain bin had been flattened. But even near-misses have ways of finding a place forever in wordless memories.

On the prairie and here on the edge of the plains, you just know when tornadoes might visit. You can feel it all day long, even when the sky is clear, the sun shining. Some kind of potent atmospheric mix sends shivers up the spine.

It's not a tornado that Asaph coaxes from his memory in these verses, but what he'll never forget—what he wants to rehearse again and again—is the perfect storm, a potent cocktail of atmospheric events that must have shaken the Israelites to the bone. There they were, the only home they'd known left far behind, when suddenly this monster storm arises. They're miles from cement ceilings, all alone on the plains.

Such storms scare people spitless. This one—the one Moses conjured himself—could not have been any different. Pharaoh and his minions are out there charging, a monster storm is brewing. Moses stands up, arms raised—and just like that, the waters of the Red Sea part, creating a dry ground walkway.

Is it any wonder Asaph wants to bring that great story back? In his anxious sleeplessness, in his worry and guilt, he tells himself to remember the Exodus story, that incredible yarn when God was there with them, miraculously, on the shore.

He wants to remember that absolutely perfect storm.

Remember? How can I forget?

Prayer

Not all of us have survived your "perfect storms," Lord. Some have perished on sea and on land, but those who've weathered the onslaught, in whatever form, are forever touched by our powerlessness. Thank you for such lessons, because they're the curriculum of all of our first-grade years. Thank you for showing us that you are God and we are not. Blessed be your holy name. Amen.

Riff

What's your "perfect storm" story?

By the Hand

‡

You led your people like a flock by the hand of Moses and
Aaron.
—Psalm 77:20

‡

Ten years ago or so, in the Netherlands, my son and I
ran into a man who asked me if I was Jewish. I had told
him my surname—Schaap—which he identified as a
particularly Jewish name in Holland.

The day before, we'd visited Westerbork, the war-time camp
and transit station where a hundred thousand Dutch Jews bade
tearful goodbyes to families and friends—and their native Holland—
on their way to Germany, never to return. The commemorative
displays at Westerbork aren't fully accessible to those who don't
read Dutch, but words aren't all that important when you're standing
alongside the tracks where cattle cars stuffed with starving human
cargo once departed for killing factories.

What I remember best about this Dutchman's assertion—that we might actually be Jewish—was the juxtaposition of Westerbork's horror with the possibility that my blood lines may have been intermingled with the horror of the war-time yellow star. My son's face made clear that he felt it too. He was just a boy.

Last night for book club I reread Elie Wiesel's *Night*, perhaps the single most famous piece of Holocaust literature. Years ago I was especially taken by the genre; I even taught a course in it. Toward the end of that semester, I hit a wall that's been with me ever since: I don't want to read any more of those stories.

But last year I spent some time once again in the throes of that horror, preparing to write the script for a documentary on Holocaust rescuers. I enjoyed that time more than I'd anticipated; but it will likely be awhile—maybe never—before I leisurely pick up another book about the death camps. I think I know all I need to know.

Last night's discussion replays oppressively in my mind this morning as I read the completion of Asaph's wondrous song of remembrance, Psalm 77. What Asaph is telling the world, in triumph, is that the remembrance of things past enables a tortured soul to see light behind the darkness. When he remembers the Exodus, God's love reruns in his imagination. When he considers the story, as all practicing Jews do during the Passover celebration, he is reminded of that divine heroism, that divine love.

Wiesel's time in the camps, his loss of his father specifically, but his whole experience of all that depravation and inhumanity, killed off the God he thought he once knew. In an unforgettable scene, when a beloved boy is hung by the SS, someone asks, "Where is God?" A voice within him, Wiesel says, answers: "Where is He? Here He is—He is hanging here on this gallows. . . ."

The purpose of Passover celebrations, some Jewish folks claim, lies in the questions that must be asked in the Seder.

The unbounded joy of the Exodus; the horrifying agony of the Holocaust. Must we select our memories? Should we? If I were Jewish, what would I want to remember? What may not be forgotten? Does obedience require silence? Are answers more important than questions?

God was there when Moses lifted up his arms. Bless his holy name. But was God at Auschwitz and Buchenwald and Treblinka and Dachau? Was God at Westerbork?

Asaph's testimony in Psalm 77 is glorious, absolutely glorious—as light is to darkness, as day is to night.

Prayer

Give us strength to remember what never should be forgotten and grace to let slip away those acts and events that are better left undisturbed. Give us wisdom to know the difference. Lay your hands upon us and give us—and our memories—your beloved peace, Lord. Amen.

Riff

When are the most horrible memories of our lives better forgotten—
if they can be? Is it easier to forgive than to forget?

Servant Fires

He makes winds his messengers, flames of fire his servants.
—Psalm 104:4

‡

The story, in Chadron, Nebraska, not that many summers past, was what the fire *didn't* take. It didn't take the town, even though it consumed huge tracts of land just south. It didn't take a life, although hundreds of firefighters, many of them volunteers, battled through 60,000 acres of pine forests and grasslands. It didn't take the spirit of the place, even though it blackened and charred some of the most beautiful landscape of northwest Nebraska.

"The fire" is something of a misnomer, because it was really five separate blazes, each of them ignited by lightning in a Wednesday night storm. No careless smokers, no untended campfire, no loony pyromaniac, no disgruntled camper—all five fires started by lightning in a tinderbox of hundred-degree temperatures, bone-dry air, and robust winds. For a time, the largest of the blazes, the Spotted Tail fire, was roaring toward town at thirty feet per second.

By Friday night and Saturday the fires had nearly half the city of Chadron evacuated and everyone frightened. The blaze took three houses but miraculously sidestepped several others before stopping on a dime behind the football field of Chadron State College—after consuming the landmark "C" hill that overlooks the town.

The fires moved so quickly and so voraciously that the curator of the town's Fur Trade Museum could do little but watch as firefighters stood guard. It was impossible for her to gather all the artifacts, but she was fortunate—as was the town itself—that the raging fire spared the place.

Three families—only three families—look today at the charred remains of their country homes, nothing but foundations. I'm guessing those three families would find little comfort in this verse of praise to God for messenger winds and servant fires.

Others, hundreds, I'm sure, offered thanks that more wasn't destroyed. Half a town, evacuated, must have bowed their heads in joy and relief when the raging flames backed off at the football field. For almost seventy-two hours in Chadron, Nebraska, it seemed clear who was on the Lord's side—it was the firefighters, battalions of them, including dozens of local construction units manning bulldozers. I'm guessing nobody sided with the flames. No one saw those five fires as servants of the Most High.

Were they?

That's the toughest question of all. Is God the author of our calamity?

I know this. The near-catastrophe drew the people of Chadron together as loving neighbors. It humbled them and made them thankful; signs around town still sing the praises of the firefighters. For three days in Chadron everything but fire management stopped and people prayed without ceasing. Go there yourself in June and visit: the "C" hill will be emerald, blooming with new life. I can make a case for the fire as servant.

But I won't—because three families lost everything. There is a time for everything, the preacher says, a time for silence too. My guess is it would take a few more years—a few more decades, perhaps—before anyone could string up a banner downtown that broadcasts this proud verse of praise.

It is amazing how broad and wide the Bible is, how unending, how amazing—not unlike the yawning Great Plains landscapes all around Chadron, Nebraska.

Only bigger. Much bigger. God's Word actually has all of our voices, and it has his. It's that big.

Prayer

Sometimes blessings appear most clearly in rearview mirrors, Lord—we know that. Sometimes what looks like horror is horror only for a time. Help us to keep in mind the eternity of your love, even when what's now and what's here seem little more than scorched earth, wreckage. Thank you for giving us words to understand your Word. Amen.

Riff

Somehow, by God's own hand, calamities can be transformed into blessings. How has that happened to you or someone you know of?

Eagles Soar

‡

The birds of the sky nest by the waters;
they sing among the branches.
—Psalm 104:12

‡

Friends of mine are excited because a couple of bald eagles, born just this spring, have returned—at least for the time being—to a pair of ancient cottonwoods on their land along the Missouri River. Mom and Dad are long gone, it seems, but the chicks have doubled back for a while.

It seems a stretch to call a bald eagle a "chick," but that's what those returnees are. Easily distinguishable from their parents, young bald eagles don't go bald—that is, they don't take on that distinguishing white head—until they mature at four or five years old. Until then, they look almost like golden eagles.

Bald eagles were placed on the Endangered Species list in 1967, but most experts believe they'll be removed soon, since their rehabilitation has been so successful. Almost miraculously they've reappeared in our neighborhood, along the Big Sioux River, every spring. They hadn't been around for decades, if ever.

This summer, in a little fishing boat on a northern Minnesota lake, I tried to get close enough to a nest to snap a couple pictures. Failed miserably, but a pair of eagles were very much a presence on the inlet where we were staying. Really, these days they're all over.

Most of us see them so infrequently that when we do, we notice. They are, like the birds of verse 14, very much "by the waters." They're huge, of course; the females (slightly larger than the males) have a wingspan as great as ninety inches and can reach a height of nearly three feet.

And they soar. My word, do they soar. Almost every North American Indian tribe includes some kind of eagle-like motion in its repertoire of dance steps, men (usually) who swoop and soar, arms outstretched, mimicking the kingly ease of an eagle's spectacular heavenly grace.

Eagles symbolize freedom as they wheel through the open skies, aloof and regal. It's no wonder we put them on our coins and fancy dancers mimic their majesty.

Not everyone likes eagles. America's best-known bird lover, the legendary John James Audubon, thought the eagle wasn't really a fit symbol of the United States. Ben Franklin agreed—"a rank coward," he said of the eagle, "a bird of bad moral character." Franklin felt the turkey would make a better national symbol. Try not to laugh.

An eagle's cry is shockingly out of character, high-pitched and shrill, seemingly panic-stricken, a sharp chirping that's unbecoming of a presence that appears so fearless. Approach a nest sometime and you'll set both parents screaming—like jays, except more soprano. They'll soar in majesty above you, but you'll wish for ear plugs. It's like seeing Billy Graham rail on his kids or Schwartzenegger squeal.

I like that. I think an eagle's bizarre voice is just fine. "Nothing can satisfy but what confounds; nothing but what astonishes is true," says Andrea Barrett in one of her short stories. Expect a scream but you get a chirp—that's OK.

I don't know if the psalmist was thinking of a pair of eagles in verse 11, but I'll tell you this—whether or not they sound the way we'd like them to, when bald eagles sit, in majesty, on the naked branch of an old cottonwood, they offer regal praise. Just sitting there, minding their own business, in silence, they're a testimony. That's what the psalmist sees and knows.

Prayer

Thank you for eagles, Lord, and thank you for their testimony. Help us to see in them the King of all creation. Amen.

Riff

Ever think of this? When Jesus wanted to call attention to the height and depth of his love for us, he didn't pick eagles—he picked the plain old sparrow. Amazing!

Your Creatures

‡

How many are your works, LORD!
In wisdom you made them all.
—Psalm 104:24

‡

'd like to think of them as ours, but they aren't—not really. Bison will be forever associated with the Great Plains, but evidence of their roaming has turned up from Florida to Alaska, from Maine to Mexico.

The common North American buffalo stands as high as six feet tall at the shoulder and may well be the best argument for vegetarianism. Strong and powerful, able to withstand extreme temperatures, a bison forages almost exclusively on grasses and sedges. Although their relatively short legs almost immobilize them in deep snow (unlike some cattle and most horses), standard size buffalo have dense winter coats that add extra layers of padding in crucial areas of their bodies in December and January.

They change their shape as frequently as Oprah, losing as much as 15 percent of their body weight during the winter, when they go into a kind of winter funk, roaming less, eating less—living, like I should, off their fatty reserves. When spring greens the prairies, they eat like fanatics and recover quickly.

Some say thirty, some fifty, some ninety—but no one will ever know how many millions used to roam the Great Plains. Why no longer? Lots of reasons, but one is more important than any other: they were in the way. The American bison was, in a sense, the soul of many Native American tribes, and as the Europeans moved farther and farther west, the buffalo, like those Native people, simply had to be cleared, like timber and the tall-grass prairie.

There are less incriminating reasons too. Not long ago I visited the Fur Trade Museum in Chadron, Nebraska, a place that celebrates a way of life long ago vanished on the plains—the era of the fur trapper, who made his bucks, basically, on beaver.

When beaver hats fell from grace among European mucky-mucks, buffalo hides became the currency in those wilderness trading posts. Eventually buffalo hunters would shoot and kill bison by the hundreds, just for their tongues. When their rifles got too hot from successive shooting, hunters would urinate on the barrels to cool them and then keep pumping lead.

It's a sad story, but, unlike the story of passenger pigeons in America, this one has a good outcome: the numbers of bison are rising these days, and their resurgence is a beautiful thing.

A few years ago, a rutting bull decided, for reasons known only to him, to run alongside the tour bus I was riding in. Just outside the windows he loped on the side of the road for what seemed like miles—ran and ran and ran and ran without tiring. A bison's windpipe is huge. Even though the average bull today weighs as much as 1,600 pounds, he's a cross-country star. The Sioux knew they'd need extra horses to run those beasts down because the American bison is fearfully and wonderfully made.

Is that spacious windpipe an illustration of God's own creative genius, or is it something that developed through thousands of years by the constant warfare we've called, since Darwin, "the survival of the fittest"?

Who cares? What we know is this: we almost killed them all, but, praise the Lord, they're making a comeback. They're rallying, even though their old world is now drawn and quartered by fences.

How many are your works, LORD! In wisdom you made them all.

Prayer

We are your works, too, Lord God. You dreamed us up and made us from the dust of the earth you created. You peopled your world with beings just like us. We've sinned, Lord, and lost some of our majesty, but you're still with us. We're marked with your image. Help us to see that image in those we know and meet, your own creation, the work of your hands. Amen.

Riff

The American bison is bountifully blessed—with huge windpipes and incredible winter coats. What about you? What are your peculiar gifts?

Sinners in the Hands
of a Happy God

‡

... may the LORD rejoice in his works—
he who looks at the earth, and it trembles,
who touches the mountains, and they smoke.
—Psalm 104:31-32

‡

Pity Jonathan Edwards.

Every year millions of bored high-schoolers, supposedly learning American literature, suffer through the tedious works of Puritan fathers and mothers, poets and essayists and historians whose combined sex appeal ranks them somewhere in the neighborhood of the old folks' home. Good stuff—good like liver and spinach.

The only voice in 150 years that comes even close to grabbing their attention is that of Jonathan Edwards, whose famous hellfire and brimstone sermon "Sinners in the Hands of an Angry God" includes some show-stopping images—like loathsome spiders dangling mercilessly over flaming pits. Those images wake kids up.

But pity Jonathan Edwards. A century of instruction in American literature has created an image of the old preacher that probably bears little resemblance to the man. He wasn't stern. He didn't pound the pulpit, didn't spit and steam or unload fear on the meetinghouse. Arguably the best mind in eighteenth-century America, Edwards was once president of Yale. He was a prolific writer and a loving pastor and father. But say his name today, and those few who recognize it hear a fearsome rant.

Maybe it's just me and my Calvinist soul, but I must admit it's somehow tougher to imagine a God rejoicing in us than it is to imagine a God angry at our shenanigans. The fuming God Edwards pictures in that sermon is easier for me to picture than the God the psalmist evokes in this verse from 104, a God who smiles, who yahoos once in a while and belts out an amen whenever he sees a kid help an old lady across a busy street.

I know something of the story of a man in town—but little of the man himself. I know he drinks far too much, so much that he can't hold a job. I know some folks around here have tried hard to help him, even though he hasn't been a jewel. Today he's parked at a rehab center where he should have been for a year or more— probably more.

I know of another man, a man who owns a salvage yard where a thousand wrecks rust and rot slowly before getting crunched up and hauled away. People go there if they need a hubcap or an engine block. The office space needs a couple of Dutch grandmas with scouring pads—it's a grease pit, unwelcoming to anyone who wasn't born with a wrench in a side pocket of his or her bibs. That's where the boss sits.

For a year now, that stoic and silent man has allowed the drunk to live in a rental place he keeps just down the street from us. No rent payments have come in because the drunk hasn't brought much money home. Just trouble. A few weeks ago, he stole a kid's bike—and that's not the half of it.

I don't know how many people in town realize that for more than a year the junkman's heart created a free home for a man few could love. I don't think the junkman would want the story told. I may be leaking something I shouldn't right now.

But if God Almighty ever high-fives his people, I swear he must be lining up in that sleazy junkyard office for a chance to do just that. He's rejoicing.

It's wonderful to think of God Almighty enjoying what we do, especially if that image is filed in the back forty of our mind, as it is in me, behind the image of an angry Jehovah.

This little verse is a gem, isn't it? And you can be sure Jonathan Edwards knew it too.

Prayer

Help each of us to be, Lord, a reason for your happiness. Give us the vision to do good, to be good, to strive for holiness. Make us instruments of your peace. Amen.

Riff

Right here, right now, write down a story of righteousness, something alive with the love of the Father, a love that is as close to
undeserved as humanly possible.

Order

He covers the sky with clouds; he supplies the
earth with rain and makes grass grow on the hills.
—Psalm 147:8

‡

They were African-American kids, and that was a big deal to this white kid who'd never met someone with black skin. They were African American, and they were from some juvenile home. When they bought a park sticker, the long-haired social worker in the front seat of the Travelall told me that the whole bunch of them had earned this trip because they'd kept their rooms clean. They had canoes. It was going to be an outing, fun.

I knew it was crazy to put those canoes into roaring Lake Michigan, but I didn't say a thing because I didn't want to be someone's old Aunt Cora.

So they took those canoes into the park, down to the beach, and into the lake. Some of them got out a ways and tipped. Four of those kids—black kids from the city—four of those kids drowned. I'd sold them the sticker. I pointed the way to the water, to their grave.

I was eighteen, and the boss chewed me up and down for not telling them it was flat-out idiotic to put those canoes in the lake. I'd grown up on the lakeshore, he said. I knew so much better.

That night I went home and told my parents—the story was all over the news. What I didn't tell them was that I'd played a role, sold the sticker.

Later that night I took out a sheet of paper. I don't know why. I took out a sheet of paper, sat at the dining room table, and wrote some things down because it seemed the right thing to do. Put it on paper, try to make some sense of it.

Writing wasn't something I was planning to do at that point in my life. So where did the impulse come from, that desire to pull out a pen and write, to talk on paper?

Almost every year I get papers like the one I wrote that night from students who are doing the same thing—writing through trauma or horror or sadness or fear. This year, a young woman described her dissolute father, a carousing, pathetic drunk. It was a bad essay but wonderful therapy. She wanted to put it down, to squeeze the memories into something she could hold in her hand, to help her see, to mark out some out some territory of her own, the way prairie settlers used to pound stakes in the grass to document their world.

Writing—even the words I'm typing right now—requires us to make sense of nonsense, to create some semblance of order out of the endless ocean of chaos. If we write, we think, maybe we can make some sense.

The landscape video in verse 8 had to be shot out here on the plains, where the sky is expansive enough to frame county-wide thunderstorms. It's not a still shot because there's a story in a single verse: clouds, then rain, then greening grass on the hills—a circle, life descending from sky to earth. Ecology 101.

God Almighty brews up the clouds, then gives them a squeeze; they weep and the earth is renewed, the emerald hills dance with joy. It's that simple. God's mighty hands order our lives. I know that.

But I keep pounding the keys, and the letters continue to appear—right now, miraculously, a blinking cursor births them one after another. I read a verse of a Psalm and try to make sense of it. I draw up forty-year-old memories from a lakeshore, a dark night in June at a family table with a single sheet of lined paper, the faces of four kids in the back of a truck. Kids who kept their rooms clean.

I'm trying to make sense of it all, trying to give it meaning.

Forty years later, I still need the rain.

Prayer

Honestly, Lord, there's a ton of things we don't get. Every day things happen that make us feel like idiots. Why, Lord? How long, Lord? Where are you, Lord? Even David felt it. Give us wisdom to make sense of things and comfort when we can't. And always grace, Lord in heaven—always, always grace. Amen.

Riff

Flannery O'Connor used to say she didn't know what she believed until she wrote about it. Try it yourself.

In the Bones

Psalms for Scribblers, Scrawlers, and Sketchers • Psalms for Scri
Psalms for Scribblers, Scrawlers, and Sketchers • Psalms fo
Psalms for Scribblers, Scrawlers, and Sketchers • Psalms fo

‡

My bones suffer mortal agony as my foes taunt me,
saying to me all day long, "Where is your God?"
—Psalm 42:10

‡

I come from a distinguished line of hypochondriacs. A minister who was once my grandfather's preacher told me that a half-century ago, when my grandfather was felled suddenly by a heart attack, an old friend of both of them appeared shocked. "Maybe he was sick—we should have believed him all those years," that friend said.

It's in the genes, I guess, although maybe I shouldn't go that far. Can hypochondria really be in the genes?

My mother has it too, as any of her kids will tell you. There's always something ailing her and has been for as long as I can remember. Doctors can never quite find it, which means she just sees more of them. My mother—bless her soul, I love her dearly—is herself a good argument for nationalized medicine.

Maybe I have it too. I'd like to think not, but who knows? When my wife and I were first married and living in Arizona, I started thinking that my arrhythmia, a condition I've had for as long as I can remember, was developing into something awful. It's embarrassing to admit it, but I was under some stress at the time, adjusting to my newly married status and unsure of myself in graduate school. Today, neither of those stresses seem all that life-threatening.

I went to see a doctor—since we'd just moved, someone I'd never seen before. He took some tests, shrugged his shoulders, and said that what I really needed was someone to tell me I wasn't sick. Which he did. End of symptoms. Call me my mother's child.

Maybe David's description of his pain in this verse is over-statement. He's trying to make a point about his spiritual anguish. It's a figure of speech. On the other hand, maybe his physical pain is hypochondria. The tentacles of his stress reach into his joints, his muscles, even his bones. He hurts all over.

Maybe depression—a deep sense of alienation from God—is the occasion for David's physical ailments. Maybe he's got thyroid problems, a frequent association. Or maybe he had some chronic pain—an old war injury—before he fell down in the dumps. Chronic pain often accompanies or even triggers depression.

My sisters and I often shook our heads in wonder at our longsuffering father, who always appeared to believe my mother's phantom pains were real. He must have learned—as we all did—that denying those pains was never going to get him anywhere because what Mom felt in her bones—physical or not—was always real.

Good doctors will admit that we are far more than the sum of our physical parts. In hospitals all over the world, miracles still happen. We call them that because we don't know—nobody does—how human will intersects with our physicality.

That's why I believe what David says, even though I'm a veteran scoffer. The pain David felt in feeling abandoned by God crept like a cancer into every atom of his being. He could feel God's absence in his bones, in his cartilage.

It's not overstatement. God seemed gone, and that pain, to David, was real—as it can be to us, hypochondriacs all.

Prayer

When pain makes life itself hard to swallow, rescue us from our abandonment. Come into our hearts with your eternal presence, and help us to see beyond the tribulation in our bones and the emptiness in our hearts. Fill us with your love. Sometimes there's so much that needs to be filled. Amen.

Riff

Not a believer in the world hasn't felt what David is feeling here, abandonment. It's a misery reserved for the faithful. How does that resonate with your experience?

Knowing How to Live

I cannot teach anybody anything, I can only make them think.

—Socrates

‡

For we are God's handiwork, created in Christ Jesus to do good works, which God prepared in advance for us to do.
—Ephesians 2:10

‡

Undouse-able

Why, my soul, are you downcast? Why so disturbed within me?
Put your hope in God, for I will yet praise him,
my Savior and my God.

—Psalm 42:11

‡

The morning is dark; the day will be cold. The northwest winds will make any foray outside something of a chore. But we've had a beautiful fall, and no one is complaining. Winter is coming. Squirrels scramble across our lawn and up our trees in anticipation, but they're fat like hedgehogs.

It's Thanksgiving Day. Upstairs the kitchen is full of empty bowls and pans and all kinds of food ready to be ladled, poured, mashed, or baked. The naked turkey, a fourteen-pounder, sits in the fridge, queen for a day. That may be overstatement—certainly it is if you're the turkey.

Six months ago, after reading an interview with Garrison Keillor, I began to take some time each day to give thanks for something—that my Dell works, for my glasses, for Walden, for the cat across the room who's snoring right now. I started this daily thanks business, betting on Keillor's idea that we could be better folks if we started our days with gratitude to God, who doesn't need our thanks as much as we need to give it.

Here's the lay of the land this Thanksgiving. My son-in-law has a new job, my daughter is happy, and the two of them love each other and their kids. Despite their ages, our parents, only two anymore, are doing as well as can be expected. Our son says there soon may be some commitment on the girlfriend front, and we're excited. And did I mention those grandchildren? They show up here and I giggle. My wife and I love each other, and we've got some blessed loons on a lake in Minnesota to look forward to this summer.

Here's what I'm thinking this Thanksgiving morning: I'm thankful that there's always something, always hope, always the dawn.

And I'm thankful because I'm like David, in a way. I know as he does that no matter how dark the day or cold the winter, no matter how impossible life might look, there's always hope, there's God the Rock. He's reason alone for thanksgiving.

Psalm 42 is maybe the most famous song of lament in the whole collection. It voices the psalmist's brokenness and despair, and I'm thankful for that, because the psalmist voiced it for all of us. That wailing doesn't appear on anyone's Christmas list, but at one time or another, in all of our lives, it's hiding somewhere behind the tree, ready to spring. I can't imagine any believer who doesn't feel the despair of Psalm 42 at some point or another in life—"Why so disturbed within me?"

But even in his despair, the poet who blessed us with Psalm 42 is as determined as a pit bull: "I will yet praise him, my Savior and my God."

I'm thankful for that double-fisted determination, thankful that my faith, while maybe not a pit bull, is at least a rottweiler. I don't understand that, and I don't know why. God has blessed me with a light in the darkness. Sometimes the light grows dim, but for some mysterious reason, it is undouse-able.

It's the gift of faith, and it's a gift of love, for which I am—this Thanksgiving morning especially—deeply thankful.

Psalm 42 is a song of triumph, even in our deepest anguish. It's a song about faith.

Prayer

Make thanksgiving a state of mind in me, Lord. Make it a way of life—as day-to-day as eating lunch or brushing my teeth. Keep me thankful because, deep down in my very soul, I'm sure that life without you would not be the joy that it is, despite our troubles. Thank you for giving me life. Amen.

Riff

For the next week, give thanks for something—anything—every single day. Try it. What about this morning? And why?

Enduring Inheritance

... and their inheritance will endure forever.
—Psalm 37:18

‡

One of the human urges behind a desire to write, I'm told, is a mostly unconscious wish to create something timeless. We want to be a Hemingway or a Dickinson, a Milton or a Shakespeare, a Venerable Bede or an Ovid. We want to speak long after our voice box has fallen away into the dust from whence it came.

Maybe. When, as an undergraduate, I stumbled upon a love of literature I never knew I had, I'll admit to believing that one of the draws of the writing life was the possibility of being included in those fat anthologies. That was before I knew the word *remaindered*, and long before I realized how many of us actually sit here, fingers curled over the keys. A friend of mine, the book editor of a major American newspaper, gets a hundred books a day to review. Those fat anthologies could be behemoth, and there's lots of competition to get inside their covers.

For the last week, I've been corresponding with two antiquarian book sellers in Amsterdam. A quarter-century ago, I stumbled on a moldy cardboard box of old Dutch books in an antique store. The woman up front told me she'd just as soon get rid of them. "Five bucks," she said, shrugging her shoulders.

Inside the box I found ancient theological books. Simply holding one is a thrill. But those old books have no vital relationship to me, even though my own DNA, on both sides of the family, wears wooden shoes. My great-grandfather came from Holland to teach theology in the 1870s; I've got many of his books too. Those I wouldn't sell. But sometime this week, one or both of those booksellers will tell me how much the books are worth, and I'll have to decide whether to ship them or put them back on the shelf.

If they are worth anything at all, their value likely derives from their age, not their authors. The most ancient was published in 1655. It's some kind of theological study—a bit smaller than a paperback, with an abundance of bronze, liver-spotted pages. It's called *De Yverigan, Christen, den Hemel door Heyligh Gevvelt: innemende.* I have only the faintest idea of what that means. I'm not even sure there's an author listed.

Most books published today won't endure like *Christen, den Hemel*—it's a matter of physics, the quality of ink and paper. I admit it—that's a bit unsettling. Somewhere deep inside I must have this jaded wish to live forever by way of the words now appearing on my screen. Fat chance!

Then there's David, whose words animate every last keystroke I'm making right now, thousands and thousands of years later. The promise he's giving us in this verse of Psalm 37 has nothing to do with his poetry or his music, or with the softly plaintive notes of his harp, the ones that calmed King Saul's soul.

The enduring inheritance David promises in this verse is nothing more or less than eternity itself, life forever, the gift of God to those the psalmist calls "blameless"—the recipients of God's own grace. We will live forever.

And that inheritance, I've long been convinced, is mine. Even if these words slip away from a hard drive or a CD after a decade or two, even if nothing I ever say lasts longer than an hour or two after lunch, eternity, by grace, is mine.

No matter what I say or write, that's an inheritance that endures. Forever.

Prayer

The only words that endure are yours, Lord—your promise, your story, and the words you use in our ears and hearts to remind us that you're there and you love us. Keep talking, and keep us listening—even if and when we seem stone deaf. May your words ever fill our hearts. Amen.

Riff

It's not only writers who want their words around long after they're gone. How about masons? Carpenters? Teachers? In a sense, I think, we all want to endure. That's not bad, is it?

A Who's Who

‡

The wicked draw the sword and bend the bow to bring down
the poor and needy, to slay those whose ways are upright.
—Psalm 37:14

‡

If the truth be known, I'm proud as a peacock. I have here beside me a fax copy of a *Library Journal* assessment of my latest book. It's a starred review that includes a short interview. Flat-out great press—can't sell books without it.

All that good stuff appears in the section titled "Christian fiction," which is OK. People who aren't interested in that genre are not likely to glance at any reviews, starred or not, that appear therein. Besides, why lie? The stories in my book come from a foundation of the Christian faith.

The reviewer commends the fact that the stories don't have, in her words, "tidy, sugary endings." In other words, my book gets a sweet review because it's not, well, typical "Christian" fiction—

fiction she obviously hates. Sure, there are some aesthetic questions involved here, but I'm not interested in those questions now. What I am interested in is my joy at being reviewed positively in a magazine that's not of the Christian community, but of "the world."

In the scenario David is drawing here in verse 14, a visual and metaphorical portrait of the Day of the Lord, the wicked are hell-bent on the destruction of the poor and upright. Quite frankly, I know which side I want to be on in that scenario. I know which side I think I'm on, and I'm not drawing a bow. I want to be among the upright, on the side of the poor.

David's description reminds me of Christ's words in the gospel of John: "If you belonged to the world, it would love you as its own. As it is, you do not belong to the world, but I have chosen you out of the world. That is why the world hates you" (John 15:19).

This morning I'm happy because a significant voice in the literary world doesn't hate me, at least doesn't dislike me the way the reviewer dislikes other "Christian" fiction. I'm feeling no pain as I bask in the admiration of the Library Journal. I rather enjoy not being hated. Should I? What does Jesus mean—the world hates us?

TV evangelist Pat Robertson once suggested that the United States should "take out" Venezuelan President Hugo Chavez. For that statement he was reviled. He was hated, although that's nothing new for him. Today Pat Robertson can take comfort from Christ's words and David's description—more than I can anyway.

Who really is "the world"? David knew—it was the pagan forces who threatened Israel, God's people. Jesus knew—it was those who would reject him (didn't everyone?), revile him, and send him to a painful death on the cross.

But I'm not always so sure, even when I see the devastation that still lingers years after Hurricane Katrina in New Orleans, a place known for profligate partying. Today "the Big Easy" is still Hurricane Katrina's cesspool. Was New Orleans an American Sodom, full of "the wicked," as some people have suggested? Was it a good idea for God to rub the place out? Is what happened there the kind of scenario David offers for our comfort?

I know that many are still suffering there today, people who need God's love and care—and ours.

Who is "the world"? Who are "the wicked"? Who are the truly righteous? The older I get, the less sure I am.

Prayer

Give us wisdom, Lord, not only to know our enemies—and yours—but to know how to deal with them. Sometimes we get mixed messages: the desire to revile the wicked and the mandate to love our enemies. Grant us the wisdom to know how to be. Amen.

Riff

Really, who are our enemies?

Vanishing Beauty

But the wicked will perish: Though the LORD's enemies are
like the flowers of the field, they will be consumed,
they will go up in smoke.

—Psalm 37:20

‡

The small town where I live has a new cinema, a five-plex, right downtown. Corporation heads somewhere else determine which films get shown, and they do so on the basis of bucks. Which films will fill the seats and their coffers? Our movies are the same ones viewed every weekend in every other city and town in this country.

No story here, right? No man biting a dog.

Maybe. Sioux Center, Iowa, my hometown, once made national news (maybe the only time) because a fiery young preacher went to war with local officials to keep movies out. And he won. I've got a *Time* magazine photograph of him holding forth, standing in front of the organ pipes in the church he was pastoring.

What propelled this pastor's agenda was his sturdy conviction—as well as the stated policy of the denomination he served—that movies were "worldly," an adjective that has since fallen almost entirely out of usage.

Magazine and newspapers are in trouble today because people get their news, information, and political opinions from television and the Internet. Print isn't doing well—except, that is, for one species of periodical—the kind that covers celebrities. People love, even worship, celebrities.

Celebrities are usually, but not exclusively, movie stars with the kinds of faces filmmakers feature in stories that often seem incidental to their beautiful images. As long as we can see gorgeous faces on our silver screens, we can make ourselves feel happy. I may sound like Billy Sunday when I say it, but today this little Iowa town sits comfortably in the American cultural mainstream with a five-screen temple of celebrity smack in the heart of things.

A verse like this one prompts me, once again, to try to identify "the wicked" among us, and it's not easy. Nonetheless, I think I can, without blushing, nominate entertainment industry fat cats who flush their bilge over the culture because they know we can't resist a pretty face. At the same time, it's only fair to point out that they wouldn't do it if we'd stay out of that main street theater. We don't, and that makes us, all of us, complicit.

I wish David hadn't used the simile he uses here, because I honestly believe that those hundreds who will go into that theater this weekend would profit far more from standing out in the fields all around us, where today the land is a bouquet of harvest colors.

David's right, of course. In a couple of months, those russet tones will be gone—just as Gwyneth Paltrow's perfect face will someday slump into the lines of mid-life.

Sic transit gloria mundi—the glory has passed, and what hasn't, will. It's a theme as old as the hills, but nearly impossible to sell, losing as it so often does to the stunning beauty that fills the screens of our theaters and home entertainment systems.

The great moral lesson of verse 20 is that some beauty is eternal. Whatever's on the screen in our small town this weekend, I doubt it will be that kind. That beauty is, well, worldly, I guess. Only eternity shines forever.

Tomorrow, as is my habit, I'll leave at dawn for those fields David cites, even though I know that soon enough it will be January, cold and colorless. Nonetheless, I know my visit will be a blessing.

Prayer

The choices we have about life are as broad as the landscape, Lord. Some of us are artists, some scientists, some couch potatoes, some just ordinary folks. Help us to know what's good for the soul, dear Lord. Help us to grow in our love for you. Amen.

Riff

For decades, evangelical Christians were more than concerned with the influence of Hollywood. For decades, "good Christians"—or so it was thought—stayed out of theaters. That era is over. Have we thrown the baby out with the bathwater? What blessings flow from Hollywood?

God's Silence

‡

When you did these things and I kept silent,
you thought I was exactly like you. But now I arraign
you and set my accusations before you.
—Psalm 50:21

‡

I listen to books during my half-hour daily workout—and I love it. Right now it's *Population 485* by Michael Perry, whose stories of small-town Wisconsin ring especially clear to Cheeseheads like me. It's a meditation, part Thoreau and part John Donne, even though Perry never talks much about his own practice of faith.

This morning, my T-shirt only half soaked, Perry's voice was rudely interrupted when another exerciser tuned the radio to Christian praise music—and cranked it up.

I never feel so much a sinner or a scoffer as when I'm in the neighborhood of Christian radio or TV. My mother says a new tape she plays daily prompts her to clench her fists and sing along "Majesty" as loud as she can. The old folks' home she lives in has thick walls, but she was always a good singer and has no complaining neighbors. She loves Christian praise music about as much as I don't. And for that I get whacked. She says I'm too comfortable with worldliness. Maybe so.

This morning I was annoyed by "Our God Is an Awesome God" because I didn't need a sermon when I was hearing a really memorable meditation from Michael Perry. Some little devil's voice reminded me just then of how much I dislike that in-your-face Christianity trumpeted over the buzz of all those exercise machines—including the bike I was on. I got into the Elijah mood, wanting to call in the bears or lightning strikes. But, good night, this wasn't just any music interrupting my reverie—it was *Christian* music (as Dave Barry might put it), music about God.

I'm not interested in blaming anyone or anything else, but the truth is, I thought of Psalm 50 at that moment—the scathing indictments, the angry blasts God himself levels on those who are adept at all the forms of righteousness and put their stock in them—like listening to a 24/7 diet of Christian music, I thought. I got petulant and angry, and much of that came, I suppose, from the still small voice of guilt.

I don't know that God Almighty wants us listening to sermons every hour of our lives. I don't think so. We've got things to do in this messy garden. But maybe I'm just trying to excuse my sin.

The scariest part of this psalm—more so than the flashes of anger God lowers on those who claim to be his—is what he admits here in verse 21: that he's kept silent about things. So maybe he was silent this morning in the middle of my anger and all that gospel noise ringing through a room with brick walls. Sometimes I wish he'd tell me if I should have shut off my MP3 player, curled up my hands like my mother, and sung "Awesome God" at the top of my lungs. Or else I wish he'd tell the guy who turned on the radio to listen to NPR. This morning five GIs died in Iraq.

"I kept silent," God says, explaining his apparent absence.

If God had broken the silence this morning, which one of us would have gotten the sermon? Would either of us?

Once I turned up the volume on Michael Perry, I was OK. In the background, of course, was "Awesome God."

And maybe that's the best I can do right here and now.

Prayer

You're not as choosy as we are when it comes to who your people are, Lord, and for that we thank you. Help us to know our brothers and sisters in your name, despite our differences, despite our dislikes and our imaginings. And please, never stop speaking to us, never keep silence. Amen.

Riff

I wonder if God can ever be distracted from his care for each of us. I wonder if he sometimes simply chooses, the way some of us do, to be alone, to keep his mouth shut.

Bewonderment

‡

Be exalted, O God, above the heavens;
let your glory be over all the earth.
—Psalm 57:11

‡

The basic paradigm by which I've always understood the Christian life is from the Heidelberg Catechism, the handbook of doctrine with which I was raised. The catechism tells a story organized in three chapters: sin, salvation, service.

The story begins with sin—our falling into sin and our knowledge of sin as it exists within us. John Calvin starts even a bit earlier, with the heavens, our sense of God as manifest in his world—what we see and experience. Because humans can't help but see God's marvelous work in the heavens and the earth all around us, we come to know that there simply has to be someone greater than we are. With that knowledge, we feel our own limitations—we aren't

God. There begins our knowledge of human limits, our knowledge, finally, of sin.

A conviction of our finiteness draws us closer to God. If we believe we are capable of fulfilling our own needs, then we have no need of a Savior. Our conviction of our limitations—of sin—is a prerequisite to knowing God's saving work. Sin precedes salvation, so the story goes.

Once we know that God loves us in spite of our sin, our hearts fill and our souls rejoice; we can't help but celebrate our salvation. That celebration leads us into gratitude and service, into being God's agents of love in the world he loves so much.

Sin, salvation, service—that's the story line, the narrative by which I was raised.

Mother Teresa's take on a very similar tale is a three-step process not unlike the Heidelberg's narrative line, but it's colored instead by her experiences in the ghettos of Calcutta. Our redemption begins in repulsion, she says: what we see offends, it prompts us to look away. But we really can't or shouldn't or won't. We have to look misery in its starving face, and when we do, we move from repulsion to compassion—away from rejection and toward loving acceptance.

But there's a final chapter—what she calls "bewonderment," which is wonder and admiration. Our compassion leads us to bewonderment.

"Bewonderment" is one of those strange words no one uses but everyone understands. I'll admit that for me, bewonderment is hard to come by, perhaps because it isn't so clearly one of the chapters in the story I was taught as a boy, the story that's still deeply embedded in my soul. "Service" is the goal of the Christian life for me, not "bewonderment."

Maybe that's why I'm envious of David's praise here. I don't think I've ever asked God to not hide his light under a bushel, to display his radiant grace from pole to pole. I'm forever asking God for favors, but only rarely adoring, in part because I'm so rarely in awe.

Bewonderment is something I'm still learning, even this morning, and for that I'm thankful—for the book of Psalms, for David, and for the God David knew so intimately that he could speak the way he did in Psalm 57.

Sometimes it's difficult to be intimate with God—a being who's so grand and seemingly out of reach. But it's something a song can teach—and the heavens too. It's something even an old man can learn, if only he has ears.

Prayer

Be exalted, Lord—be the almighty King of creation. Shine over the world and all its hordes of people. Write your name in the heavens and open our eyes. Bring us close, bring us near, bring us to you like the father you are. Amen.

Riff

How long has it been since you've been filled to the brim with bewonderment?

Great Gods

✠

Your ways, God, are holy. What god is as great as our God?
—Psalm 77:13

✠

I t couldn't have happened to sweeter people. A group of thirteen social workers, Missouri state employees who work for the Department of Social Services Family Support Division/ Child Support Enforcement in Florissant, Missouri, claimed a $224.2 million Powerball jackpot—the largest prize ever won in the Missouri Lottery. About $8.5 million apiece after taxes. Not bad for a five-dollar bet.

I don't play the lottery or hang around casinos. My wife and I walked into one several years ago—the Winnebagos just south of here. We divvied up twenty bucks in tokens, played the slots, and walked out fifteen minutes later, twenty bucks poorer. Haven't been back to the bandits since—and likely won't.

I'm not self-righteous about it. I've eaten in lots of Great Plains reservation casinos, and I often giggle at the irony—dozens, even hundreds of descendants of European immigrant folks tossing their bucks at Native people. Don't tell me God has no sense of humor.

I do fantasize, however. What if I'd won five million dollars last week?

Trust me—I'd blow this pop stand. I'd buy a Minnesota cottage, a place big enough for a study overlooking some gorgeous reedy lake. With loons. We'd have to have loons—wouldn't buy the place unless I could hear them. I'd need a boat, not a big one, just big enough to get out on the water when I wanted to. I'd write and fish and clip the grass, trim the trees, keep up the flowers. We'd eat perch and walleye and maybe a bass snagged from a weed bed along the shore. My wife would love it.

It would be hard for us to move from this house, the one we've been in for twenty years. But once I signed the lease on that lake home, I'd be packing. I have a hundred thousand things I'd like to write before the vision goes. I'd start working once the computer was set up in that new office, the one with the windows.

"What god is as great as our God?" Asaph asks.

Easy for him to say. He lived in Israel, around 600 B.C. What did he know about beer-batter walleye or a half-dozen perch? What did he know about the haunting cry of the loon, the solitary pleasures of trolling a fishing line in the water the moment the sun clears the eastern horizon?

It's a rhetorical question. Asaph doesn't mean for us to quibble because the answer is axiomatic. "Why, no god is as great as our God. What a dumb question."

Wish it were as easy as that. But the fact is, siren gods try to woo us from faith in our Maker, and too often they succeed—not because filthy lucre is itself that glorious but because it offers us our dreams. Money puts a roof on our fantasies.

Believing in God isn't all that difficult. In fact, spirituality is hot today. Faith itself, it seems, is something of a "must have."

But a life of holiness is a much tougher sell. Every moment of advertising preaches a different gospel, and we hear it continuously. There are other gods, and they're nothing to shake a stick at.

If it weren't so, there'd be no more casinos, no more lotteries, no more Minnesota dreamin'.

Prayer

Most of our aspirations are caught somewhere between what we need and what we want, Lord. It is a mark of our sin that we dream as gloriously as we do. Give us peace—more than anything, keep us satisfied, content, at ease. Forgive us when we go chasing other gods, for no god is as great as you. Amen.

Riff

I don't think it's wrong for me to dream, to wish I had a Minnesota cabin. So when do our dreams become gods?

Our Shield and Our Anointed One

‡

Look on our shield, O God;
look with favor on your anointed one.
—Psalm 84:9

‡

The first person to use the biblical phrase "a city on a hill" in the United States was John Winthrop, one of one of the very first writers in American literature and governor of the Massachusetts Bay Colony. He used it in "A Model of Christian Charity," a sermon he preached before he even arrived on these shores. Ronald Reagan quoted it in his second inaugural address, and many others have used it too. The association Winthrop created with that sermon—that somehow the United States is favored by God Almighty—is the water in which American kids swim, the air they breathe. We are, we're quite sure, a chosen nation, blessed by God.

Throughout history, the marriage of nationality and religion has often been destructive—probably because patriotism and faith draw on emotions so deep that they may, from a distance, seem almost one and the same. On Memorial Day (what we used to call Decoration Day), my grandmother wouldn't miss the annual "doings" in the local cemetery—color guard, marching band, a sermon by some local pastor calling us all back to God, and then, finally the mournful reverence of "Taps." My parents often didn't feel like going, but they did—Grandma demanded it. She expected attendance because our fallen boys needed to be remembered. One of those fallen was her only brother.

Whether or not this country is in a profound moral crisis is always worth a good discussion, but these days many of my fellow believers are confident the whole nation needs to be grabbed by the collar and dragged back to its Christian roots. John Winthrop was a Christian, but 150 years later, at the time of the American Revolution, most of the movers and shakers were deists who could rather easily shrug off Christ's divinity. The notion that the United States is, or ever has been, "chosen" like Israel, or even "Christian," is myth. But then, myths are nothing to sneeze at.

Not long ago, my denomination dropped a hymn that was a favorite of many members because the tune, by Josef Haydn, was the same as the German national anthem. Our denomination's rich contingent of post-World War II immigrants from the Netherlands simply could not sing praise to God with the music because they kept hearing "Deutschland Uber Alles."

This particular verse from Psalm 84, an incredibly beautiful psalm—Spurgeon calls it "one of the choicest of the collection"—is something of a roadside bomb. "Look on our flag, Lord," one might paraphrase, "and think of our president." That's an understandable interpretation, and I don't doubt my grandma prayed that prayer during two long and terrible world wars. But her devotion doesn't make the sentiment any less fearful, because we are no more a "chosen nation" than is Dominica or Iceland.

Winthrop, who, along with his Puritan compatriots, was interested in establishing a theocracy, could not have seen that.

I'm not sure about Reagan, but I don't think Grandma could have understood that equation either. Her only brother missing for almost a year in the trenches of France, she might have asked, "Shouldn't we be praying that way too?"

I know the answer to that question, but I'm not sure how I would have been able to answer it.

Prayer

Lord, guard us from wrapping you in the colors of our flag; protect us from believing that you are somehow on our side in all skirmishes and battles. Help us to become more deserving instruments of your peace. Allow us to be your hands, and keep us pure in all things—loyal first, always, to your kingdom—not the kingdoms of this world, not even our own. Amen.

Riff

These days it's easier to get in a fight about "American exception-alism" than it has ever been since the Vietnam War. How is it that so many Americans believe that the United States is somehow a "Christian nation"?

Knowing Where We're Going

We know what we are,

but know not what we may be.

—William Shakespeare

‡

"For I know the plans I have for you," declares the LORD,
"plans to prosper you and not to harm you,
plans to give you hope and a future."
—Jeremiah 29:11

‡

Evil Empires

Psalms for Scribblers, Scrawlers, and Sketchers Psalms for Scri
Psalms for Scribblers, Scrawlers, and Sketchers Psalms for
Psalms for Scribblers, Scrawlers, and Sketchers Psalms for

‡

The wicked plot against the righteous
and gnash their teeth at them. . . .
—Psalm 37:12

‡

According to Human Rights Watch, in the highlands of Vietnam today Protestant Christianity is growing fast, a fact that does not go unnoticed by the ruling Communist regime, which sees the Christian faith—and its growth—as an enemy to their authority.

Because Christianity is deemed a threat, the government has banned churches in many villages, kept preachers out of their congregations, and made sure worship is closely monitored. It has even mandated that successful applicants for certain jobs must openly reject Christianity. According to the Human Rights Watch report, "Confidential government directives . . . show a centrally directed national campaign and special bureaucratic infrastructure to target and suppress Christians in ethnic minority areas in the Northern and Western Highlands."

Not long ago, three housewives in Indonesia faced the possibility of five years in prison for directing a Sunday school program they called "Happy Week." The women were charged when a devout Islamic school principal heard Christian songs being sung by kids walking down the school's hallway.

When the court proceedings were held, militants packed the courtroom and screamed for death for the defendants. There was no proof that the children were coerced into attending "Happy Week." In fact, their Islamic parents frequently accompanied the children on field trips.

I am far less a citizen of this world than I should be. It's almost impossible for me to imagine a place in which one's faith could be the cause for persecution and death. But there are places right now where it is—and where David's assertion in this psalm rings as true as it did for him, plagued as he was by those who would bring him down. There are many places in the world where the wicked, their teeth gnashing, plot against the righteous.

A quarter-century ago, who would have ever have guessed the world would spin into the direction it has today? The Enlightenment— the assumption that religious faith was a remnant of our barbarism and would eventually fade into oblivion—is history, some say. It was dead wrong. In fact, the world's most incendiary battles are religious in character today. See for yourself.

People in the modern, secularized West—me included—blush at David's rhetoric in this verse, but in some quarters, David's sense of things sounds sadly familiar.

Some people say that verses like this should grab our attention because we may well be coming to a time when—as is true in many so places—the verse seems not a whit anachronistic.

I remember a preacher friend saying to me, years ago, during a particularly upsetting situation in the church where he was serving, that after ten years in the ministry, nothing really surprised him anymore.

Who knows what the future will bring? Someday this verse may sound the same to me as it does today to the people in Vietnam or Indonesia, in Iraq or Saudi Arabia.

May the Lord our God be with us. May the Lord bless us all with peace.

Prayer

You've told us that there will always be wars and rumors of wars, but their frequency or constancy don't make them any easier. Help us all to be, like Jesus, instruments of your peace. Amen.

Riff

Is persecution a part of your life in any way at all? Who's gnashing their teeth at your holiness?

Bridegrooms

‡

In the heavens he has pitched a tent for the sun,
which is like a bridegroom coming out of his chamber. . . .
—Psalm 19:4-5

‡

I wasn't the one who said it—it was my friend.

We were high up on a rise in the northernmost reaches of the Loess Hills, that quirky set of miniature mountains that runs nearly all the way up the western border of Iowa, when, just as we knew it would, the sun emerged from its gaudy pavilion. My friend's a fisherman, so he's seen it before—must have thought about it, I guess.

"Reminds me of the passage in the psalms—the bridegroom, the morning after," he said, chuckling.

I'd never thought of this verse before, honestly, and I'd certainly never examined the reaches of the simile in exactly that way, the sun as a newlywed husband who's just had one great night.

Right then, at that moment, the sun coming up before us, it seemed the only way to unpack the simile. I laughed, not because it was a joke but because I'd been a bridegroom, and so had he.

I suppose it's important to add that there's a female version of the simile as well. But this male/female thing is a distinction that I'm creating, and no one else—and it's sure to make somebody mad. What the heck.

There are times—plenty of times—when how we understand a metaphor or how we interpret a poem, a story, a Van Gogh painting, or a Beatles tune says as much about us as it does about the work itself. A child's reading of Psalm 23 is history once that child reaches adulthood and looks at the psalm closely again. Things look different to different people. Our different views make criticism both a joy and a necessity.

So far, so good, right? But here's the rub.

Let me repeat: there are two ways of understanding Psalm 19's sexiest simile—one of them is male and the other is female. You've already heard the male version: the sun steps forth smilingly, proudly, from his honeymoon chamber. That's the image the two of us were chuckling about in the Loess Hills.

But there's another way of reading the simile that puts the honeymoon *ahead* of the bridegroom, not behind him. The second interpretation—the one I'll call female—is a picture of the bridegroom just about the enter the chapel, perfectly groomed and tuxedoed, spit-shined and ready to meet his bride. In what I'm calling the female version, the psalmist is referring to the prenuptials; in what I'm calling the male version, the psalmist is referring to the afterglow.

Who's right? That's a fray I'm staying out of. But I'll tell you this, I've been to enough weddings to validate what I was thinking years ago when my wife and I got married (and I'm only somewhat embarrassed to say it): Let's get the hoopla over and the consummation underway.

I'm the one who chuckled when my friend looked up at the rising sun and thought of the morning after. Made perfect sense to me.

But I won't lay our version on you. You'll have to choose for yourself. Either way, it works.

Either way, dawn is a joy. And that, after all, is what the psalmist means.

Prayer

Lead us to the dawn, Lord—help us to see your handiwork, your artistry, your immense power and glorious design, not only in the morning, but all day and all night long. Keep us near, always. Amen.

Riff

Which interpretation do you prefer?—the bridegroom going to the bridal chamber, or leaving it?

Covenant

‡

[The righteous] are always generous and lend freely;
their children will be a blessing.
—Psalm 37:26

‡

Most people in our church wouldn't think it was a proper worship if we didn't do "joys and concerns," an open-mike opportunity for people to air their grief, list their needs, and announce their happiness. The weekly event has become sacramental—it wouldn't be a stretch to say that for most of our congregation, it's an identifying characteristic of our fellowship. It's part of how we're *us*.

Some stubborn questions arise in me about this ritual, and not just because only certain joys and concerns ever get mentioned—after all, some problems are entirely too personal. Some folks never get any air time because their timidity keeps them seated, while boldness animates others to the point where we hear them fortnightly. What's more, I'm always cautious about public righteousness—but maybe that's just my problem.

My biggest hesitation about this way of praying, however, is the fact that "joys and concerns" is almost entirely supplication, which may well be the least significant aspect of communal prayer in worship. But I know sound like a professor. I've been wrong before, and I'd likely be banished from the fellowship if I ever dared say publicly what I've just said here.

Besides, good things happen too. We rejoice with births, we cry with those who watch their spouses go to war, we know and feel others' heartaches—some of them, at least. Going public has definite rewards, and I'm no longer itchy about it. Sometimes I even enjoy it.

One woman asks for the microphone and offers a similar petition about once a year, in part because she, like other parents, carries the burden week after week, while others' plights and exaltations come and go. She stands in the middle, where she and her husband sit, and asks in a slightly quavering voice if the congregation would remember all those children of the fellowship who aren't living in faith.

No Christian parent is ever joyful about raising that concern, no matter how constantly it weighs on the heart, and this woman is thinking of herself when she says it—everyone knows that—but she's also thinking of others, probably more than a few.

David's promise in this verse isn't hollow, but neither is it definitive. Who can forget the priest, Eli, whose sons were a holy terror? David himself had a boy who in blind lust raped his half-sister. And then there's seditious Absalom, ready to kill his own father. His life ended when he hung by his hair from a tree. David was heartbroken.

So why does David say what he does in this verse? It wasn't even true in his own life, for pity's sake. Who's he trying to convince?

Maybe, just maybe, he's trying to convince people like the woman who stands up annually to ask us to remember all our wayward sons and daughters. She holds, tooth and nail, to "covenant" theology, the idea, as Spurgeon says, that "the friend of the father [and/or mother] is the friend of the family."

That's the only comfort in her—and our—heartache. That's what we have to hold on to when there seems so little else.

King David, the world's foremost poet and singer, sometimes wrote better than he knew. That's certainly one definition of inspiration, I guess.

Prayer

Lord, be with every last parent who's worried about his or her child, no matter how old that child. Bring our loved ones to faith. You can do it. You've done it before. Bring our children home, please. Amen.

Riff

They are, after all, the only pieces of this life we'll take with us to heaven, people say—our children, that is. They're all we'll have from here.

You Will See It

‡

Hope in the LORD and keep his way. He will exalt you to
inherit the land; when the wicked are destroyed, you will see it.
—Psalm 37:34

‡

Yesterday's news spoke the unvarnished truth. While violent crime may be down all across this country, it's not hard to see at least one reason why: the United States ranks first in the world in the percentage of populace serving prison time. What's more, we're 25 percent ahead of the next-highest. We've got millions of people—well over two million, in fact—behind bars.

But the real story was a kid from Chicago who'd been a passenger when another kid in the same car murdered someone in a drug mess. Just fifteen at the time, he hadn't pulled the trigger, hadn't aimed the gun. Today, at twenty-nine, he has no chance of parole from the cubicle he's lived in for fourteen years.

When I heard that story, I was entirely convinced of the injustice created by a system that doesn't seem to believe in rehabilitation. That is, until a mother was interviewed, someone whose little boy had been brutally murdered. That woman said that if her son's murderer were released from prison, she would scream. It's not difficult to understand why.

I still think the kid shouldn't have to be incarcerated forever, but when murderers are convicted justly, everyone celebrates. Real perpetrators need to pay for crime, violent or white-collar. And I believe it's a good thing for the victims of crime, like that mother, to have a last word with those who have altered the course of their lives.

I just don't care to see it. Some moments in our lives shouldn't be offered to an audience. While victims may well need to scream, we don't need to hear it, despite the fact that allowing victims' families the opportunity to address criminals must give those who've suffered some significant satisfaction. "Closure," some people call it.

What David promises the righteous in this long psalm is justice. Look around, he says; the wicked always prosper. But someday things will be reversed—that's what he keeps saying. With this verse, however, he pushes even farther: "You will see it," he says. With your own eyes, you'll see the wicked wiped out. You'll take joy in their demise.

"Vengeance is mine, says the Lord," the Bible says elsewhere. And whenever we take vengeance into our own hands—even though the motivation is understandable and maybe even therapeutic—it's just not pretty. It doesn't show human character at its best.

But I get what David is promising here. Almost five years of Nazi occupation of the Netherlands ended in the Starving Winter, when hundreds of people died of starvation. Then, in early May of 1945, the Nazis were vanquished when Canadian troops poured into a country that had been tortured for almost five years. Just imagine the ensuing celebration of that liberation—still a holiday every year in the Netherlands. It must have been immense.

In this verse David promises joy—not vengeance. He promises the pure intoxication of longed-for liberation—nothing less than redemption.

With your own eyes, he says, you'll see it. That, I'll watch.

Prayer

Until that day, Lord, help us to love our enemies, to do good to those who don't seek our good, to smile through our adversity. Help us to love as Christ himself taught us to love, unceasingly. Fill us with your grace. Amen.

Riff

Sometimes the Bible is a tough, tough book. How do you square this kind of assurance—that we'll see the wicked destroyed—with Christ's command to love our enemies?

How Lovely

✝

How lovely is your dwelling place, LORD Almighty!
—Psalm 84:1

✝

t's silly to make the argument—there were countless other factors—but historians who know the Sioux Indian wars often point to a Mormon cow as the cause for a half-century of horror on the Great Plains. In August 1854 that cow, belonging to a Mormon party moving west, wandered into a Brule camp and was killed.

The owner demanded restitution. Lieutenant John L. Grattan, who had little or no experience with American Indian tribes, insisted on arresting the killers and led a group of thirty infantrymen to the Brule village. When the culprit refused to turn himself in, Grattan turned his howitzers on the people. Chief Conquering Bear was killed with the first volley, but the Brules wiped out the entire detachment. And so began the Sioux Indian wars.

Although Psalm 84 is an all-time favorite for many, strangely enough, it's the Mormons who come to my mind. That's because when I consider their grand narrative—the long overland trek from Nauvoo, Illinois, to the basin of the Great Salt Lake in Utah, a pilgrimage that began in 1846, eight years before that wandering cow—I feel something of the exuberance that marks this very precious psalm.

The story of the Mormon exodus is a purely American story, just as Mormonism may well be the first truly American religion. From 1846 to 1869, seventy thousand Mormons traveled west to a place where they believed they could live in peace and freedom, insulated from persecution they'd suffered wherever they'd lived before. And they were right.

Hundreds, even thousands, pulled handcarts, walking the entire thirteen hundred miles. They had a goal, a destiny. They wanted a place to worship, a place to live their own pious vision. That shared goal, I'm guessing, gave them the strength and dedication, the sheer will to endure every last horror the plains and mountain passes could throw. Along the way, they improved the trail, knowing others would follow.

Daily life was strictly regimented: the Mormons knew that chaos and infighting would be the death of them and of the enterprise. Each day they read Scripture, prayed, and sang together. It was a massive, dangerous, difficult pilgrimage, and it was successful. Once they'd safely arrived in Salt Lake City, their incredible journey became a story that would be told for generations.

The incredible joy of Psalm 84 arises, I think, from similar long and difficult pilgrimages, exacting journeys of faithful believers to a beloved place that is both of this world and of the next. A wagon train of worshipers on their way to a city that is, in a way, celestial.

"How lovely is your dwelling place," the psalmist writes, almost as if he were, in effect, wordless. Sometimes I wish I could feel that kind of ecstasy about the weekly worship I attend, but I don't believe we're talking about similar rituals. It's pilgrimage that evokes the delight that makes this hymn ring through the ages, pilgrimage, in the oldest sense of that word, a vivid spiritual journey.

Even a dead cow is part of that story, an altogether too-human story of religious aspiration and, finally, glorious arrival. That's why this psalm reminds me, somewhat enviously, of the Mormons.

If it's difficult to imagine the triumphant joy of the singer in Psalm 84, consider the Mormons. Imagine their joy. Then consider this vale of tears, and imagine the loveliness of an eternal dwelling place. That too can make us sing.

Prayer

Someday, when our life's hour is over, bring us home, Lord, to that dwelling place you've carved out of the rock of ages, the rock of your grace. Bring us home. Bring us home. Amen.

Riff

This world is not my home, says the old song. But this world provides the only real definition we can feel of "home." Why is home so good?

". . . But in Battalions"

Deep calls to deep in the roar of your waterfalls. . . .
—Psalm 42:7

‡

first heard the line years ago from my wife's grandmother, who
I knew only for a few years as a rather elegant woman with a
radiant crown of silver hair. I don't remember the occasion,
but I'll never forget the comment because it seemed so out
of character for a fine old Christian matriarch. "When bad things
happen," she said, eyes almost averted, her head shaking slightly,
"they always come in threes."

I had no clue where she got that idea, nor why she believed
it. Grandma Visser, whose people were hearty Calvinists for
generations, could not have pointed anywhere in Scripture for that
notion, as she could have for most of her foundational beliefs. But
this ancient bit of folklore—does it have pagan roots?—never fully
left her psyche, even though she probably read the Word of God

every day of her life. "Bad things happen in threes." She wasn't—isn't—the only one to believe it. Google it sometime.

Can it be true? I don't know that anyone could do the research. But for generations of human beings who've been caught in the kind of downward spiral David must have been in when writing this song, it seems like a valid perception. And as often as not, perception creates its own realities.

Is it a silly? Sure. If we expect it to be true, we may be silly. But maybe its longevity argues for some ageless relevance. Whether or not it's true isn't as important, perhaps, as the fact that, strange as it may seem, it has offered comfort and strength to human sorrowers.

This much I remember from Grandma Visser: she fully expected something more than she'd already gone through, some additional misery. She had counted two; she expected another. Simply by repeating the old line she was strengthening herself for the journey, steeling herself for the next sadness, anticipating that three would mean the end. My guess is that ancient folk wisdom finds a place in the human psyche not necessarily because it's true but because it's comforting: it brings order to the chaos of our lives. There are three, and that's it.

Interesting, I think, that Eugene Peterson uses the word *chaos* in his version of this verse: "Chaos calls to chaos," he says. He's just as right as anyone, I suppose, for it's impossible to claim biblical inerrancy when it comes to a verse like this. The King James Version uses *waterspouts* where the TNIV says *waterfalls*, wholly different phenomena. Nobody really knows what specifically is meant by "deep calls to deep."

And yet everyone does, everyone who's faced a march of consecutive sadnesses. "When sorrows come, they come not single spies but in battalions," Shakespeare says in *Hamlet*—an even more depressing assessment than Grandma Visser's.

We don't know the specifics here, but many of us understand the sweep, the intent. There are times when our lives feel like Thomas Hardy novels—things simply seem to get worse and worse and worse, not better.

There are no vivid pictures embedded in the line "deep calls to deep," but that doesn't mean most of us can't find ourselves in its meaning.

We can't avoid the painful reality of the soul that's sliced opened to us in Psalm 42: the singer who believes in the Light but sees nothing but darkness around him.

And maybe—thankfully?—the outlines of a third bad thing.

Prayer

For those already reeling from loss and sadness, Lord—and there are many—bring relief. Take them up in your hands, for your strength is all some have or hope for. Grace us with the conviction that there will be an end to sorrow, a dawn of joy, of heaven itself. Amen.

Riff

When has that bit of ancient folk wisdom—bad things always come in threes—seemed true to you?

When?

‡

My soul thirsts for God, for the living God.
When can I go and meet with God?
—Psalm 42:2

‡

The Ghost Dance, one of the saddest religions of all time, was a frenetic hodgepodge of Christianity, mysticism, Native ritual, and sheer desperation that swept Native life throughout the American West in the final years of the nineteenth century.

Wovoka, a Piute holy man, saw the original vision and then designed the ritual from his own revelation. Erect a sapling in an open area—a familiar symbol from rituals like the Sun Dance, which was, back then, outlawed by reservation agents. Purge yourselves— enter sweat lodges, prostrate yourself before Wakan Tanka, the Great Mysterious, to witness to your humility. Warriors would often cut out pieces of their own flesh and lay them at the base of that sapling to bear witness to their selflessness.

Then dance—women and men together—dance around that sapling. Dance and dance and dance, and don't stop until you fall from physical exhaustion and spiritual plenitude. Dance until the mind numbs and the spirit emerges. Dance into frenzy. Dance into religious ecstasy.

If his people would dance like that, Wovoka claimed, Christ would return because he'd hear their prayers and feel their suffering. And when he came, he'd bring the old ones with him, hence, the "Ghost Dance." The buffalo would return, and once again the people could take up their beloved way of life. If they would dance like that, the dust from the new heaven and the new earth would swallow the *wasicu*, the white people. If they would dance like that, their hunger would be satiated, their thirst assuaged, their sadness comforted.

"The great underlying principle of the Ghost Dance doctrine," says James Mooney, "is that the whole Indian race, living and dead, will be reunited upon a regenerated earth, to live a life of aboriginal happiness, forever free from death, disease, and misery." It was that simple, that compelling a vision.

As a white Christian, I am ashamed to admit that in the summer of 1890, the desperation of Native people, fueled by poverty, malnutrition, and the near death of a culture, created a religion that played a disturbing role in the massacre at Wounded Knee.

Many of us who read the opening two verses of Psalm 42 have never felt the thirst David is talking about. So it's helpful for me, a white Christian, to know the story of the Ghost Dance, to understand how thirstily Native people looked to a God who had seemingly left them behind. Their people were dying, spiritually and physically.

That's why the thirsty four-legged creatures, the deer of Psalm 42:1, would have made great sense to Native people. Back then, they would have understood the opening bars of David's song.

Because what's at the bottom of this lament is nothing less than God's apparent absence.

When contemporary Christianity turns excessively therapeutic and promises something Disney-like, something smilingly insipid, lines like these can be read as if they were nothing more than words. But humankind has all too abundant a history for that.

I'm not at all thankful for the story of the Ghost Dance, or of David's own desperation recorded in this memorable psalm. But I am comforted in the knowledge that when my bootless cries seem to disappear into the wide-open spaces of the plains where I live, I know I'm not the first to feel abandoned. That's how David felt too.

The gift of grace in the near despair of the opening lines of Psalm 42, or so it seems to me, is that we are never really alone.

Prayer

For being beside us each day, Lord, help us each day anew to offer the thanksgiving of our very lives. You promise that you will not leave us thirsty, as amazing and sometimes even doubtful as that seems. You will ever be our God. Thank you for that blessed assurance. Amen.

Riff

Hunger feeds desperation, even when the hunger is metaphor and has nothing to do with the stomach. We do strange things when we're desperate.

Heavenward

Psalms for Scribblers, Scrawlers and Sketchers Psalms for Scrib
Psalms for Scribblers, Scrawlers and Sketchers Psalms for
Psalms for Scribblers, Scrawlers and Sketchers Psalms for

‡

For great is your love, reaching to the heavens;
your faithfulness reaches to the skies.
—Psalm 57:10

‡

Those of us who are Christians have a hard time not thinking of heaven as someplace "up." Jesus Christ "ascended," after all. Jacob saw a vision of a ladder descending, and Elijah boarded a chariot that departed for all points upward.

That upward proclivity of ours results, at least in part I suppose, from some ancient Platonism in early Christian thought. It's the idea that this world is somehow less than sweet, and we've got to leave it behind like our old natures before we can ascend to something, well, heavenly.

People have said there's nothing above us for miles and miles. *Nothing* is overstatement, of course. All sorts of planets and stars and whole solar systems are up there, so many that astronomers have never located a dead end sign.

I have theologian friends who claim that the new heavens and the new earth really mean that heaven will be right here on earth. It's just that we'll have no more hog lots. Everything on *terra firma* will be unspoiled—like the Garden of Eden, only with all the best of human culture thrown in too. We won't be one big eternal choir; instead, we'll employ ourselves as we do now, maybe, only there'll be no backaches or seat belts.

I don't think David is being metaphorical here, although he is using his official poetic license. I think he's talking about the sky, not angelic heaven. The Old Testament patriarchs weren't obsessed with heaven the way we are. Last week I saw a pick-up with a license that spelled TNKHVN, and I understood at least something about why they call those tags "vanity" plates.

But I don't think David is talking about heaven, per se; he's settled on the greatest expanse of *infinity* his finiteness can locate—the skies. Saturday morning I went out with the camera, the first clear Saturday in a month, to find the skies crystalline. A cold wind had swept away dust and fog, and the sky was tinfoil bright and shiny.

Just as we need sin to make stories, camera bugs out here on the plains need clouds to create a photograph when the skies are as everlastingly wide as they are here. But then, David is not toting a digital in Psalm 57. He's just praising the Lord, and what I'm thinking is that *this* sky—not a particularly good subject for photography—but *this* sky, the one where there is absolutely and blindingly nothing, with the sun not a disk but a huge burning smudge of colorless luminescence, is the one he's seeing or imagining.

That kind of sky goes on forever—and now I'm making metaphors. That kind of sky seems as limitless as he wants us to imagine.

But then, the literal subject matter of this verse is not the sky but God's love, which David says, like last Saturday's skies, simply can't be contained. In his ecstatic praise, he reaches for the only comparison he can imagine, and there's just nothing as endless here below as a perfect crystalline sky.

But even the sky—that limitless sky—is no match for God's love. The heavens, even when they appear to stretch out forever, can't compare. And even the world's most famous poet can't stretch words that far. Like all of us, tongue-tied as we are, David is just doing the very best he can.

Someday we'll all have new vocabularies. I'm not sure where we'll be, but we will have the words to make sense of what's now so immensely far beyond us, the miracle of God's love.

Prayer

Thanks for the heavens, Lord—both day and night. Thank you for giving us the sky, the only measure of eternity we can perceive here in your own handiwork, your creation. But thank you even more for your love—which is greater, wider, fuller, truly never-ending. Amen.

Riff

What's your picture of heaven? What will you be doing?

Songs in the Night

I remembered my songs in the night.

—Psalm 77:6

‡

We were standing in an old country church in South Dakota with tin ceilings. There had been some additions: two wings on either side of the front, far enough to fit in an extra two rows of pews. The carpet was new, the paint fresh, but the place was, and still is, ancient, by prairie standards at least. It's 120 years old, and no matter how diligently its people keep the place up, the lines of the old frame church still show its age.

My immigrant great-grandparents once walked weekly through those same front doors, then sat with their five kids beneath those tin ceilings. I've got a history in that old church—that's what I was thinking that day. Even if I'm the first great-grandchild, the first descendant in two generations ever to darken the front door, part of me is here.

We'd just come from an exhausting day along the Missouri River—some hiking, some sightseeing—and we were stopping at this nondescript country church in the middle of a town well along the road toward dying. It was early June, and beautiful—the sun was radiant, and the emerald land we'd been driving through seemed empty of distraction and, honestly, full of God.

I don't know where the hymn came from, but it bubbled up in my soul from somewhere in my childhood. I never considered it a favorite and hadn't thought about it for years or sung it for decades. Long ago it was chased from the hymnal by more peppy stuff, I suppose. What came to me that day was a perfectly fitting opening line aboard a haunting melody that seemed written for this time and place.

So I asked my fellow tour bus travelers whether they remembered "To the Hills I Lift My Eyes" from an old psalter. Average age was sixty-ish. They shrugged their shoulders, but that was enough of an assent, and besides I wasn't about to be thwarted. So I started in, grabbing a pitch out of nowhere, and soon enough they were all with me, because the first line hadn't left anyone's memory and it's a very simple melody—Psalm 121.

As a group, we patched the lyrics together because some of us knew enough of the lines so all of us could get through it without missing a beat.

The bright sun outside suggested the threat of midsummer heat; there was not a whisper of night in that church just then. Even so, when I hear Asaph's voice in this verse—"I remembered my songs in the night"—I think of that moment in the old church. It was the blessedness of connecting with something so much greater than me, or us, or any of our individual stories, something so ethereal that the only way to express it was through song. I don't know that I understand how and why, but sometimes beatitude is palpable in such unreasonable things.

Those of us who believe know the distinct comfort of faith, a comfort that begins in the fulsome sense of our belonging—to Whom we belong.

There's no doubt about Asaph—he was a worrier. But here in Psalm 77, he's telling us that the remembrance of things past— especially the memory of what could only be expressed in song— was itself a testimony to the end of sadness. Asaph's remembered songs in the night didn't end his sadness—just read on. But all that beauty reminded him that once, at least, there was joy.

And if once, then why not again?

Prayer

Thanks for your psalms, Lord, and what they tell us about the writers and the millions of people who've taken them into their own souls for thousands of years. Thank you for giving us, in your Word, ourselves, our very natures, our experiences. Thank you for all of your songs in the night—and all day long. Amen.

Riff

You don't have to be a musician to know that sometimes music expresses things that can't otherwise be said.

Not to Be Continued

But all sinners will be destroyed;
there will be no future for the wicked.
—Psalm 37:38

‡

I believe there will be an end to the world as we know it, but, unlike Jerry Jenkins and Tim LaHaye, not to mention millions of others in America today, I have no idea what that end will look like.

Years ago it was Hal Lindsey, a prophet who still has a website, even though I thought *The Late, Great Planet Earth* had all the believers delivered by 2005—lock, stock, and barrel—to the right hand of God, the earth ensnared in pre-Armageddon politics or already aflame. He was sure that "the bear" in some minor prophet had to be Russia, which meant we were on the brink of the last days. Today Russia is a cub. I'm not sure exactly what Lindsey was forecasting, and neither do I care. All I know is he sold a ton of books. There's always a market for end times.

After Black Sunday, that Sunday in the thirties never to be forgotten by old-time Great Plains residents, the day the first of the dust storms arose like some great black fist in the western sky, lots and lots of good, God-fearing folks, sand-blasted suddenly into farming oblivion, were convinced we were not all that far from "the end."

It's not difficult to understand why. A woman I know told me she'd never forget that day because she was in church—afternoon service—when the dust first rolled in. In a matter of minutes the dust was so thick that all she could see was the pastor's white collar. Is it any wonder people looked up? No one could see a hand before a face.

Today new natural calamities appear weekly—record hurricanes in the Gulf of Mexico, thousands dead in earthquakes and floods and tsunamis. That people would look to God as a deliverer makes all kinds of sense. It's a joy to imagine an end to suffering, to know the Lord won't tarry.

Prophets of doom, like the poor, we will always have with us, even though history has proved their never-ending scenarios of doom—every one of them—as bogus as swamp gas.

Of course, some American Christians say the same thing about about abortion too, and gay marriage, and evolution in schools. They say these are all signs of the times, that this world's curtains are coming down. When the sky is falling and the faithful seem few, the last trumpet can sound far more comforting than fearful.

My mother goes there too, so occasionally I need to coach her out of it. But who knows? Maybe thirty years down the pike, when I'm pushing ninety, I'll be listening intently for a blast of that horn myself.

In this long psalm of bellowing confidence, David can't stop singing about how good it is to know that the righteous are loved and the wicked aren't—about how just rewards are given to those who do—and those who don't do—the will of God.

Someday, I assume, because I believe, one of the folks with the crystal balls will get it right and the world will end. Not because it was predicted, but because the Creator of heaven and earth wants it done.

David isn't wrong. Someday—maybe even this afternoon—every last knee shall bow. That I believe.

Prayer

Lord, we know that someday all of this will end, although none of us knows exactly what will happen. What we do know—what we can be sure of from day to day—is that your love will see us through, no matter what happens. Thank you for abiding with your people. Amen.

Riff

For centuries believers have misread what the Bible calls "the signs of the times." Will we ever get it right?

Deliverance

‡

They spread a net for my feet—
I was bowed down in distress. They dug a pit in my path—
but they have fallen into it themselves.

—Psalm 57:6

‡

Two thieves enter a convenience store with evil on their minds. They threaten the attendant, and while one of them, the guy, helps himself to the bucks in the till, his accomplice—and probably girlfriend—spots a contest entry form—who knows what for?—and proceeds to fill it out, dreaming of a big win. They leave, but the form includes her name, address, and phone number. Doesn't take the cops long to get to their apartment.

A bank robber in the northeast uses a standard M.O. He lugs a bag into the bank, claims it's a bomb, cleans out the cash drawers, and leaves the bag, telling the cashiers that it's going to explode. The bags he uses are often filled with books—who knows, maybe even one of mine. His undoing comes the time he leaves a phone book in one of those bags, a book he'd been mailed, complete with his address. The jig's up.

I don't know whether David was chuckling a bit to himself when he thought of the cartoon irony in verse 6—probably not. The first half of the verse recounts his deep distress: "I was bowed down." But there's a kind of Keystone Cops comedy to what he describes next—those enemies plotting and scheming, only to become victims of their own nastiness. Stripped of its immediate context, what happens when evil turns inside out is a joy—and sometimes funny.

And not just funny either. When things like that happen, people have been known to utter profound theological truths: "Aha, there *is* a God." When sinners get theirs, especially when the "getting" is done at their own hands, it just feels good—all is right with the world, chaos is flouted, righteousness reigns. We look up and hear the music of the spheres.

Psalm 57 could hardly have been written in the middle of the drama. It has to be a testimony, really. David's opening-line distress— "Have mercy, have mercy"—is short-lived. In verse 4 he documents the evil character of King Saul's posse, but the anguish of that first line soon appears not to have been uttered at all. Here in verse 6 we get the whole story, which means the heartfelt cries of the first verse are really history. What had once happened tested him, David says—or sings—but that anguish soared into triumph when those dolts, oddly enough, became the victims of their own hijinks.

It is a peculiar joy we all feel, or so it seems, when providence takes control in our lives. David's deliverance isn't hard-fought here, as it sometimes is. At this point, it seems, he barely has to lift a hand—or that's what he tells us.

Saul's boys dug a pit into which they themselves fell headlong. Isn't that a riot?

God did it—the whole thing. It is worth a chuckle to be audience to God's own jumbo sense of humor. May God's name be praised—that's David's testimony in the rest of Psalm 57. They got theirs. Thank you, Lord.

A man with a shotgun came after the owner of a Chevy Camaro, wanting the vehicle. The owner got out, scared. The car thief jumped in, grabbed the keys, and then realized he couldn't drive a stick shift.

It feels so good when all is right in the world. Bless God's name.

Prayer

Lord, replenish our souls with a good laugh once in a while, and a smile, especially when we come to understand and see that those who hate you are not left to roam through the world at will. Take evildoers out at the knees, Lord. Every once in a while help us to laugh at a good old pratfall. Amen.

Riff

Sometimes, it seems, evil goes unpunished, but most often, the bad guys get theirs too.

Clothed with Gladness

✝

The grasslands of the wilderness overflow;
the hills are clothed with gladness.

—Psalm 65:12

✝

t's hard to estimate just how long it's been since the world
outside my door offered much to a landscape photographer.
Snow can be gorgeous, but we've had less than enough to
create the alabaster robes that make the plains look regal.
Ever since the first killing frost, the country here has been almost
entirely monochrome, colorless.

The color is not gone, really, but, the fields outside of town
look a good deal less than spectacular. I'm understating here. Less
than inspiring. Shoot, inspiring is a stretch. From December through
late March the world I live in is dull, plain, uninteresting, dreary,
colorless—yeah, all of those. This winter, the dawn's early light—

always a blessing—has been rare on those few days I can get out to look. Saturdays, more often than not, have been cloudy and dreary.

Photography is all about light. Manure glows like a blessing in the golden joy of sunrise, but spot a perfect composition in heavy clouds and no matter how you fine-tune a digital file, what you've got is almost unfailingly uninteresting. Fogs cast a spell, but a prairie winter has few mists worth noting.

We're thick into the season of "Farch," a coinage of February/March, when the snow that remains is flat-out dingy. Last week's sudden blizzard left long and heavy drifts asleep in the ditches, but, they look, a week later, like dead sheep, as Jim Heynen once wrote, gray lifeless masses that will stay around way too long once the sun decides to shine.

If I made my living as a photographer who didn't roam, I'd starve. My winter shots hardly merit the space they take up on my hard drive. I could delete the whole bunch and not miss a thing, really.

Last Saturday a storm was forecast, so I assumed there would be no dawn. But when I stepped outside early, the clouds were broken enough out east to allow the weary sun at least a bit of stage time, so I took off and found some old cottonwoods out of town, some fallen. I thought I had some fine shots until I got them up on the screen. Nothing to write home about. Maybe it's my fault. There's a learning curve with my high-tech gear, and I'm too old for new tricks and too blasted male to read the instructions.

Dawn lasts ten minutes, maybe fifteen before the patina fades. I need to remind myself that this is the season of Farch—nothing striking anywhere. Saturday my wife brought home a clutch of tulips that just about took my breath away. It'll be awhile. I'll just have to wait.

The earth rests, the fertile, slumbering soil beneath us hibernating. It'll have toil enough in a month or so when farmers start to work it once again.

It's Farch and it's Lent and it's too cold to be spring, even though today, officially, is spring solstice. In South Dakota there's eighteen inches of snow, which is enough to prompt the old Midwestern adage "Things could be worse."

There will come a moment, a time, a succession of months, in fact, when the hills out west are as clothed with gladness as the ones David saw rejoicing and singing. There will come a time when the grasslands overflow.

Patience is a virtue. Hope is a thing with feathers. Faith is the sure knowledge of things hoped for. I'd better be ready. I've got time now to read instructions. Emeralds will return, refreshingly. I know it. I can hear the promise in the song.

Prayer

Thank you for the change of seasons, Lord, always an inspiration. Thank you for spring especially, for the moment when life emerges once more, and especially for the day of resurrection. Amen.

Riff

Come October, even winter starts to look good out here on the edge of the Great Plains. What we do without seasons?

Questions

✝

My heart meditated and my spirit asked:
"Will the Lord reject forever? Will he never show his
favor again? Has his unfailing love vanished forever? Has
his promise failed for all time? Has God forgotten to be
merciful? Has he in anger withheld his compassion?"
—Psalm 77:6-9

✝

I knew the couples up front. Three of the four of them had been my students at one time or another. Grandparents and uncles and aunts—some of them from far, far away—held honored places on adjacent chairs. For both couples, the baby they were holding was their first, and those two towheads were also both first grandchildren on both sides of both families. Pride may well be the root of the deadly sins, but our church sanctuary last Sunday morning was overflowing with it, and there wasn't a dime's worth of guilt.

If those fathers had ever shown as much concentration in their writing as they did that morning when the preacher drenched their babies' foreheads, they would have had far less trouble in my classes than they did. Their focused attention on their babies and the sacrament was a blessing—simply the way they were attuned to what was going on was a revelation.

I don't know why, but when the baptisms were over and both couples were standing in front, husbands holding the babies, we sang "When Peace, Like a River," an odd hymn to sing right then, given its history. It must have been by request; I doubt our preacher would have chosen it. My guess is that it was someone's favorite.

I can't sing that song without getting choked up because of the story of Horace Spafford, who wrote that hymn after losing his four daughters when the ship they were in went down in the Atlantic. But that's another story.

The sacrament was glorious, the music resplendent. Last Sunday morning in our church there was good reason to be overwhelmed with God's grace.

But just beside me sat a couple who, a year ago, suffered the loss of a four-year-old grandson, who one Sunday walked away from his father for just a second, fell into a creek that was a bit swollen, and was never seen again, his body never recovered.

The proud reverie of a pair of first-time parents up front made those grieving grandparents beside me dig out Kleenex. There I sat, somewhere, like all of us, poised between heaven and hell.

Most good writers say rhetorical questions are sophomoric, a cheap way to incite interest. In these verses, Asaph lines them up like dominoes, one after another—six of them. When read together these questions feel less like toys than like the consecutive blows of a murderous cudgel. Aspah's beating away on God's chest. "Are you there or not?" he's demanding—brash and impudent and pushy—even sophomoric, I guess, just like all of us.

In the barrage of questions Asaph spits out, I feel what I felt sitting next to those bereft grandparents last week in church, their anguished muffled breaths, their tears—especially in the very tumult of joy all around.

What I know from sixty years of life—and from a single worship service just last Sunday, is that Asaph is not alone.

God never promises a rose garden, only his presence, and when that presence seems an absence, we're all sophomores, I suppose. There's nothing but questions.

Prayer

Some people never really get over difficult losses, Lord. Be with them when the rest of us have long ago forgotten. Be near unto them when, once again, even years later, they feel so very much alone. Comfort them with your peace and your love. Amen.

Riff

Sometimes we feel hamstrung between joy and sorrow. How is that they come together so often?

The Work of Our Hands

Psalms for Scribblers, Scrawlers, and Sketchers Psalms for Scrib
Psalms for Scribblers, Scrawlers, and Sketchers Psalms for
or Scribblers, Scrawlers, and Sketchers Psalms for

‡

... establish the work of our hands for us—
yes, establish the work of our hands.

—Psalm 90:17

‡

The bike path east of town cuts diagonally through tall fields of corn that sometimes buffer the constant prairie winds and sometimes channel it. Yesterday when the temperature was a hundred degrees, that narrow corridor acted like a wind tunnel, so that I fought it all the way down, then sailed along when I came back to town.

Dry corn makes noise. Its leaves get stiff and curl up lengthwise, then crack against each when they get bullied by the wind. I've never been a farmer, but I've lived beside twelve-foot corn most of my life, and I know when to get worried. We haven't had rain for far too long. Three weeks ago, I stopped mowing when our lawn turned to toast. From a distance, a section of corn still looks emerald, but up close it cracks.

The man who planted the tall corn corridor around the bike path died this summer. My wife told me about his death weeks after it occurred. Had I known, I would have gone to the funeral. Once, years ago, that man told me I ought to write a book about his life. He was right, but I never did.

Cantankerous and quarrelsome, this guy deserved a book. We'll call him LeRoy to protect his memory—not because he was ever innocent. His wife left him after a couple decades of what must have been horror. For a time, fistfights with his son were public spectacles. Once, a neighbor's sow wandered on his yard. LeRoy shot it dead, and then called the neighbor to pick it up. That neighbor called the radio station to nominate LeRoy for "Good Neighbor of the Day." The whole town laughed when he got it.

For a time, we both went to the same church. A friend of mine told a friend, a Lutheran, that our church would pay for the new sanctuary the Lutherans were building if they'd take LeRoy in the bargain. "Thanks, but no thanks," the Lutheran said.

There's more. Lots more. There should have been a book. Later on in his life, he mellowed, thank the Lord.

Yesterday—and every day I take that bike path east of town in this heat—it bothers me that there's no one around to worry about that corn. I know LeRoy would, but he can't, and he's not. I feel somehow responsible, if that makes sense. LeRoy always liked me; I'm not sure why. Lots of folks, he didn't like. Whenever I ride my bike through that tunnel of tall corn and hear its leaves cracking, I feel somehow sad for him. He ought to be there to worry, like farmers do.

Like I worry about a bunch of things—my children, my mother, my work. I've got no tall corn this drought-ish July, no crops to worry about, no cattle to feed and keep cool. But I've got my concerns.

Like Moses and like LeRoy, I'm sure, I often pray that God Almighty will establish the works of my hands—these very words I'm typing. Don't let 'em dry in that hot sun, Lord. Keep 'em growing and green.

This cry of Moses arises from the pain of a heart estranged, a man whose thirsty soul has been languishing in the eerie darkness of an eclipse hiding God himself. Here Moses is asking that what he does with his hands, what he does from day to day, his work, his toil, his care—that all of that be blessed. That's all he wants. That's what most of us want.

What Moses wants is good corn to feed a hungry world.

Prayer

May the words of my mouth and the meditation of my heart be pleasing in your sight, O Lord, my Rock and my Redeemer. Amen.

Riff

"Establish the work of our hands" is such a wonderful prayer. What would you like God to establish?

His Word

‡

He has revealed his word to Jacob,
his laws and decrees to Israel.
—Psalm 147:19

‡

Most of the mornings I've worked at Psalm meditations in the last five years, I've read a little Charles Spurgeon first, followed closely his wonderfully aphoristic comments on all the psalms in huge work he titled *The Treasury of David*, three volumes, a set a bookstore owner gave me years ago, assuming, I guess, he'd never sell them. *The Treasury of David* has been a boon, a joy, a revelation all its own.

Verse by verse, Spurgeon takes each psalm apart and riffs, tells readers, in his peculiar nineteenth-century voice, what he thinks about every last line from the songs. Spurgeon is in many of these meditations too, even though they're my own.

After spinning his own takes, Spurgeon cuts and pastes a section of comments from others he's appreciated in a section titled "Hints to Preachers." For Psalm 147, comments come from John Trapp, Genebradus, A. S. Aglen, J. N. Pearson's *Life of Archbishop Leighton* (1830), Christopher Wordsworth, J. J. Van Osterzee, William Bates, Thomas Manton.

I don't know a single one of them. But there are enough to make me know I've not been plowing new ground in these meditations. How many millions have read the psalms? The only way to appreciate the numbers is by God Almighty's sands-on-the-beach or stars-in-the-sky metaphors. Billions, literally.

It's still dark out this morning. The little basement window above my head reflects the light from inside this mess not even I would call an office. But I just returned from the gym, and the sky is patchwork, which means that the dawn, soon to arrive, could be another masterpiece. The sun rises late this close to solstice, but often in a blaze. I may just grab a camera, go out, and hunt for this morning's recitation of glory.

We've got sky out here on the edge of the plains. We've got more sky than any of us knows what to do with—more heavens to declare God's glory, to preach and sing his presence. He's here and he's huge. I hear his proclamations daily, I swear.

But I've also got this cloud of witnesses, Spurgeon and friends, to show me how they sang the psalms—good coaching, maybe a little museum-ish, but heartfelt, thoughtful, and pious men, often more so than I am. Without them, I wouldn't have made it.

And I've got the Word, the book of Psalms itself, David and Moses and who-knows-who else. I've got the skies and I've got the songs, the world and the Word—day-in, day-out reminders of what God does and what he says. What a blessing.

In Psalm 147, David's panoramic vision closes down with verse 18, and then he goes on to say that those who love God are witnesses, not only to what God does but also, just as gloriously, to what he says. We've got his Word.

Not long ago, I found the old bookstore owner's picture online among the list of local sex offenders.

But if I've learned anything from slugging through the psalms in the last five years, it is that God is far greater, far more loving than any or all of his readers—Spurgeon, Schaap, and sex offender.

Our God has given us his Word and his world. Even more amazing, he's given us—sinners, all—his love. Count me among them, but count me too among the blessed.

Prayer

Lord, thanks for this book of Psalms. Thanks for everything it says, everything it tells us, and everything we read into it because we know it was written by people just like us—the same hurts, the same joys. Thanks for giving us our own presence in your Word. Amen.

Riff

What's your take on the Psalms?